# WOMEN WHO KILL

(3 BOOKS IN 1)

RAMPAGE KILLERS

TEENS WHO KILL

&

NURSES WHO KILL

SYLVIA PERRINI

PUBLISHED BY:

GOLDMINEGUIDES.COM

# Copyright © 2013

Sylviaperrini.goldmineguides.com

All rights reserved.

No part of this publication may be copied, reproduced in any format, by any means, electronic or otherwise, without prior consent from the copyright owner and publisher of this book.

This book is for informational and entertainment purposes. You do not have permission to distribute, resell, trade or barter, or give away this eBook without the expressed written consent of the author/publisher. The author or publisher will not be held responsible for the use of any information contained within this eBook.

## DISCLAIMER

In researching this book, I gathered material from a wide variety of resources, newspapers, academic papers, and other material both on and offline. In many cases, I have referenced actual quotes pertaining to the content throughout. Although the author and publisher have made every effort to ensure that the information in this book was correct at press time, the author and publisher do not assume and hereby disclaim any liability to any party for any loss, damage, or disruption caused by errors or omissions, whether such errors or omissions result from negligence, accident, or any other cause.

## TABLE OF CONTENTS

# FEMALE RAMPAGE KILLERS      1

BRENDA ANN SPENCER      4

PRISCILLA JOYCE FORD      18

SYLVIA WYNANDA SEEGRIST      27

LAFONDA FAY FOSTER and TINA HICKEY POWELL      47

LAURIE DANN      56

JILLIAN ROBBINS      75

JENNIFER SAN MARCO      81

AMY BISHOP      91

SABINE RADMACHER      106

CONCLUSION      110

# TEENAGE GIRL KILLERS      115

JULIET HULME AND PAULINE PARKER      117

CHERYL PIERSON      148

HOLLY HARVEY AND SANDRA KETCHUM      166

CHELSEA O'MAHONEY      180

| | |
|---|---:|
| CINDY COLLIER AND SHIRLEY WOLF | 185 |
| ALYSSA BUSTAMANTE | 194 |
| PROZAC | 209 |

## NURSES WHO MURDER — 212

| | |
|---|---:|
| MARIE JEANNERET | 214 |
| MARIA CATHERINA SWANENBURG | 222 |
| JANE TOPPAN | 224 |
| AMY ARCHER-GILLIGAN | 229 |
| BERTHA GIFFORD | 234 |
| Marie Fikáková | 249 |
| CECILE BOMBEEK a.k.a. Sister Godfrida. | 254 |
| "LAINZ ANGELS OF DEATH" | 257 |
| GENENE JONES | 263 |
| BEVERLY ALLITT | 289 |

# FEMALE RAMPAGE KILLERS

The definition of the difference between a spree/rampage killer from a serial killer is subject to considerable controversy, and the term is not consistently applied. The Federal Bureau of Investigations (FBI) defines a spree killer as a person (or more than one person) who commits two or more murders without a cooling-off period. This lack of a cooling off period, according to the FBI, marks the difference between a spree killer and a serial killer.

Dr. Michael Stone, a professor of clinical psychiatry at the Columbia College of Physicians and Surgeons in New York City who wrote *The Anatomy of Evil,* has examined the minds of spree killers and says,

"People usually don't commit mass murder more than once. Usually you're dealing with an angry, dissatisfied person who has poor social skills or few friends and then there is a trigger that sets them off. The precise knowledge of what makes these people tick is harder to come by than in a case of a serial killer who is studied very carefully by psychologists on the defense and prosecution teams."

Michael Stone added that 96.5 percent of mass murderers are male, and the majority isn't clinically psychotic. Rather, they suffer from paranoia and often have acute behavioral or personality disorders. In some cases the perpetrator, like that of mass murderer James Huberty who, in 1984, shot dead twenty-one people and wounded nineteen others at a McDonald's in San Ysidro, California, harbors a severe grudge or murderous feeling toward someone. James Huberty had been fired from his job not long before the incident.

Of the roughly 200 mass murderers whom Stone has studied, only twenty-five were ruled clinically insane. The others were generally angry loners or social misfits who were then "tipped over into ungovernable rage by some event."

The identity of a serial killer is normally unknown until he/she is caught. Police usually know the identity of the spree/rampage killer while his/her spree is being perpetrated, and he/she is sought after as a fugitive, commits suicide, or is shot while committing the crime. To try and understand the mind of a spree/rampage killer, try imagining yourself committing this kind of heinous crime in a public school or other public place. The majority of us can sooner imagine being among the dead or injured rather than being the killer—which just demonstrates the complexity and rarity of the killer's mind.

When one thinks of spree killers or rampage killers, normally one thinks of a male. Men such as the Aurora Colorado Movie Theater James Eagan Holmes, Seung-Hui Cho Virginia Tech

Massacre, Columbine school killers Eric Harris and Dylan Klebold, Adam Lanza at Sandy Hook Elementary School, and the 2011 massacre at a summer camp in Norway, by Anders Behring Breivik to name just a few.

Yet, women have also committed these crimes just not in such large numbers as men.

Welcome to the world of the Female Rampage Killer.

# BRENDA ANN SPENCER

Brenda Ann Spencer was born on April 3rd, 1962 in San Diego, California to Wallace and Dot Spencer. Wallace and Dot had three children together: two boys and a girl. Brenda was the middle child.

They lived in the San Carlos neighborhood of San Diego, a largely rather ordinary middle-class area of the city. Most of the houses in the neighborhood were built in the late 1960s and early 1970s, in the popular Ranch Style. Over the years, owners had added second stories and patios, giving each house its own individual look. The Spencer family home on Lake Atlin Avenue stood opposite the public Cleveland Elementary School.

Brenda's father Walter was an audio-visual expert at the nearby San Diego State University. He was also a keen hunting enthusiast and kept a collection of guns in the family home. On the weekends, he would take the children out to shoot birds and tin cans.

When Brenda was nine, her parents divorced and the father won custody of the children. The divorce had a detrimental effect on

## BRENDA ANN SPENCER

Brenda, and she became withdrawn. When her mother, Dot, left the family home, she made little effort to keep in touch with the children.

At the age of sixteen, Brenda gave the outward appearance of looking like a normal teenager of that era. She was about 5'1" tall, slender, and had long, bright, red hair parted in the middle; however, she was far from attractive. She had a large nose, dead eyes, and wore glasses. She had few, if any, close friends and would frequently play hooky from school.

For Christmas in 1978, Wallace, her father, bought Brenda a semi-automatic .22 caliber rifle with a telescopic sight and 500 rounds of ammunition. On January 29, 1979, after her father had left for work and her brothers had departed for school, Brenda played hooky again and looked out of her bedroom window. Across the street, she watched as young schoolchildren began to line up outside the gates of Grover Cleveland Elementary School as the principal, Burton Wragg, walked across the playground to unlock the gate.

Brenda then went and from under her bed pulled out her rifle. She carefully loaded it with ammunition and then positioned herself by her window and took aim through the telescopic sight. Brenda began randomly shooting at the children across the street.

Meanwhile, Principal Burton Wragg, having returned to his office after unlocking the gate, was finishing his cup of coffee with teacher Daryl Barnes when the two men heard what they thought were firecrackers going off,

"Pop, pop, pop."

Burton Wragg rushed from the room and out into the playground while Daryl Barnes headed for the side door into the playground. As he rounded the side of the building, he saw the principal bending over a crying child lying on the ground. Suddenly, Burton Wragg spun around and stumbled backwards into some bushes, as a red stain spread across his chest.

Daryl Barnes hastily grabbed a couple of children and pushed them into the school building as he yelled to the secretary to telephone the police. He then raced back outside to pick up another injured child and heard more shots ringing out. Daryl tried to calm the panicking children and as he did so he saw the janitor, Mike Suchar, racing towards the principal with a blanket in his hand. Before Daryl could call out a warning to Mike Suchar, the janitor spun and cried out,

"My God, I've been hit."

Across the road Brenda continued shooting on and on,

"Pop, pop, pop…"

Just before 9am, the police arrived at the school in response to the telephone call from the school secretary. Brenda shot one police officer, Robert Robb, in the neck. When the police identified where the shots were coming from, they moved a garbage truck in front of the school to obstruct Brenda's line of fire, barricaded the neighborhood, and deployed a SWAT Team. The uninjured children were removed from the back door of the school, and ambulances carried the injured to the San Diego Alvarado hospital.

In twenty minutes, Brenda had shot: Principal Burton Wragg, the janitor, Mike Suchar, Police Officer Robert Robb, and eight children ranging in age from seven to ten. The scene at the Alvarado hospital was bedlam. Children were crying, and others were too traumatized to whimper. Hysterical and frantic parents filled the hallways, calling out names, demanding to know from the overworked staff if their children were there.

There were two dead, Principal Burton Wragg and the janitor, Mike Suchar.

Meanwhile, Brenda had barricaded herself in the house. As news of the appalling, senseless massacre spread, the media descended. One astute journalist from the *San Diego Tribune* telephoned the Spencer home. Brenda answered and freely admitted that she was the one doing the shooting. When he asked her why she told him,

"I just started shooting. I just did it for the fun of it. I just don't like Mondays. This livens up the day. Do you like Mondays? I have to go now. I shot a pig [policeman] I think, and I want to shoot more. I'm having too much fun to surrender."

The police began to negotiate with megahorns for Brenda to

surrender. Brenda, in response, said she was only going to "come out shooting." During the following six hours as the world looked on shocked and horrified, Brenda made various comments to the police who were trying to converse with her.

When Brenda was asked if she was aiming for anyone in particular, she said it was random but that she rather liked,

"Blue and red jackets and especially liked shooting the ones wearing down jackets so she could watch the feathers fly. It was just like shooting ducks in a pond. It was really easy pickings. It was a lot of fun watching the shot children and seeing them squirm."

During another conversation she said,

"I had no reason for it. The children looked like a herd of cows standing around; it was really easy pickings."

For six and a half hours, Brenda Spencer refused to surrender to the police. Then, suddenly at 3:30p.m., as if she no longer found it fun, she laid down her rifle and surrendered.

When Brenda's mother, Dot, was informed over the telephone by the police of her daughter's arrest for shooting several people and asked to come down to the police department, she reportedly replied,

*"I can't go. I have a table full of money."*

# BRENDA ANN SPENCER

*Brenda Spencer*

When the police searched the Spencer house, Police officers found beer and whiskey bottles cluttered around the house but said Brenda did not appear to be intoxicated at the time of her arrest. They also found the rifle, in excess of 200 rounds of ammunition, and forty empty shell casings. They described the house as filthy.

Brenda was taken for toxicology testing but no traces of drugs or alcohol were found in her system.

In the ensuing weeks following Brenda's arrest, neighbors claimed that Brenda was a troublemaker, had a history of drug abuse, petty theft, truancy, and had a reputation for torturing cats. They said she was a frumpy, skinny, tomboyish, shy girl and that she was "deeply unhappy that her mother wasn't around."

Classmates at Patrick Henry High School recalled that the week before the shootings, Brenda had said that she wanted "to do something big to get on TV." They also said,

"She was always talking about guns and bragging about the guns her father had."

They said she was far from popular at the school. Her classmates also claimed that she expressed a negative attitude toward police officers and had talked about how she was going to shoot one.

Prosecutor Andrea Crisanti backed up this claim saying,

"We interviewed a friend of hers who admitted the two of them had been planning to kill someone for some time. They decided they wanted to kill a cop to see what that would feel like."

In 1979, British musician Bob Geldof was visiting the US when the news of Brenda and the school shootings hit the news. He then penned the now famous song "I don't like Mondays."

He said in an interview that he found,

"Not liking Mondays as a reason for doing somebody in is a bit strange. I was thinking about it on the way back to the hotel, and I just said 'Silicon chip inside her head had switched to overload'. I wrote that down. And the journalists interviewing her said, 'Tell me why?' It was such a senseless act. It was the perfect senseless act, and this was the perfect senseless reason for doing it. So perhaps I wrote the perfect senseless song to illustrate it. It wasn't an attempt to exploit tragedy."

The song was first performed less than a month after the massacre and became a hit in the UK in July of 1979. Brenda's family attempted unsuccessfully to stop the record from being released in the United States. Consequently, San Diego radio stations refrained from playing the track in respect to local sensitivities surrounding the shootings.

Brenda pled guilty to two counts of first-degree murder, eight counts of assault with a deadly weapon, and one count of an assault on a police officer.

Brenda, due to the seriousness of her crimes, was tried as an adult but because of her age she escaped the death penalty. In 1980, she received a prison sentence of twenty-five years to life in the California Institution for Women in Chino, California. Since she has been incarcerated, she has been diagnosed as an epileptic and suffering from depression.

Brenda became eligible for her first parole hearing in 1993, when she was thirty-one. She told the parole board that at the time of the shootings, she was under the influence of drugs and alcohol and that the state prosecutors and her attorney, Michael McGlinn, had conspired to hide her drug test results. She also alleged that the state authorities had conspired against her by putting her on mind-altering drugs during her hearing and for two years after. According to Brenda, she had not realized that she had pled guilty to the charges due to the drugs.

## PAROLE HEARINGS

The parole board took just fifteen minutes to reach a decision and deny her parole.

At Brenda's parole hearing in April of 2001, Brenda, now age forty, said that she felt like she was a different person. She also told the three-panel parole board that,

"I live with the unbearable pain every day of knowing that I was responsible for the death of two people and caused many others physical and emotional pain and suffering, but I'm not a murderer. I know saying I'm sorry doesn't make it all right. I wished it had never happened. With every school shooting, I feel I'm partially responsible. What if they got their idea from what I did?"

The parole board then asked Brenda about her famous comment "I just don't like Mondays."

Brenda replied,

"I can't remember saying it. I'd been drinking and taking drugs and don't remember much from that day. I was hallucinating and thought I was shooting at commandos storming our house. I only remember talking to negotiators."

She was then reminded that she told a negotiator,

"It was a lot of fun seeing children shot."

Brenda then, for the first time ever, claimed her violence grew out of an abusive home life in which her father beat and sexually abused her. When asked why she had never discussed these allegations with counselors, Brenda replied,

"I had tried to but, they generally ignored me."

Richard Sachs, the San Diego Deputy District Attorney, said that,

"Her behavior in prison shows she isn't ready for freedom. After the recent breakup of a relationship between Brenda and another woman inmate in prison, she heated a paper clip and used it to carve onto her chest the words 'courage' and 'pride.'"

Brenda replied,

"It was just a tattoo."

Richard Sachs claimed,

"It showed an inability to deal with stress and an inclination to act out in anger."

Brenda's parole was unanimously denied.

When Wallace Spencer was told during an interview that Brenda had claimed he had sexually abused her, he was clearly shocked stating,

"She what? Brenda said that? It's not true. No, that never happened. I would take a lie detector on that!"

### Parole Hearing September 27,

At the 2005 parole hearing, Brenda, now age forty-two, was almost unrecognizable from the sixteen-year-old adolescent arrested almost twenty-five years earlier. She was almost grandmotherly in looks, obese, and looked much older than her age.

The prosecutor argued that Brenda should not be given parole as the act was planned, and she had behaved with,

"Sniper-like behavior, in a deliberate manner, and with callousness on her part out of boredom and rage and at no time had she shown any sense of guilt."

## BRENDA ANN SPENCER

Brenda said,

"I don't remember doing it. I'm sure I did it. I don't remember it, but I'm sure I did it."

She again claimed that she had been drinking and hallucinating and said she was "basically I was trying to get myself killed." She went on to describe herself as a "screwed-up kid" who had problems at school and was highly suspicious of others. Brenda again claimed that her father had sexually abused her. The parole board asked for details of specific incidents. She replied that she remembered being hit, called names, and being yelled at and then, almost as an afterthought, she stated that her father almost raped her and that he had touched her inappropriately.

The parole board then questioned her about her father's visits to her in prison. She replied,

"We've gotten to be friends."

Brenda's brothers do not support her claims of abuse.

Brenda also said that she was "deeply sorry" for the harm she had caused the victims and their families, but she remembered only "bits and pieces" of that day and didn't remember the shooting itself. The parole board then asked Brenda if she had any plans if paroled. Brenda said she had marketable skills,

"I like to drive a forklift."

This is a job she then had in prison.

Parole was denied.

Brenda, now age forty-seven, had a fourth parole hearing on August 13th, 2009. The parole board again denied her parole, and she will not be eligible to apply again until 2019.

Even today, the children who survived Brenda's rampage, as adults, struggle to understand why it happened. Christy Buell, who was hit in the buttocks and stomach and has a foot-long scar from two operations that saved her life, remembers that,

"It felt like my whole body was falling asleep, like pinpricks all over."

She saw the principal falling into the bushes and could hear someone yelling,

"Run! Run!"

## BRENDA ANN SPENCER

She crawled up a pathway where a teacher heard her crying and pulled her into a doorway as two more bullets flew over her head into the door. Despite this, Christy believes Brenda has served her dues and should be freed; she is the only one of the survivors that does.

The school closed down many years ago but a small bronze plague still sits at the foot of a flagpole in honor of the two men who died that day: Principal Burton Wragg and the janitor, Mike Suchar.

I find it very strange that Walter Spencer still lives in the same house where his daughter, with the gun he had bought her, committed her rampage. If Brenda is granted parole, is this the house she will return to? Wallace Spencer has usually maintained a public silence about Brenda's crime other than saying,

"I was devastated. It blew me away. I fell apart myself. I don't feel responsible. I love my daughter, and I want to see her get out of there and be able to take care of herself. I don't know. I can't explain why she did it."

Since Brenda's rampage that cold January day, similar headlines and news reports have now become numbingly familiar. What was once thought unimaginable: that a school, where we send our child to be educated and protected, can become a killing field is, sadly, a grim reality today.

# PRISCILLA JOYCE FORD

Priscilla Joyce Ford was born on February 10, 1929 in Berrien Springs, Michigan.

In 1957, despite having above average intelligence, she only obtained a high school education. She managed to secure a job as a teacher in a small school in Dowagiac, Michigan. She kept the job for nearly eight years and was known as a caring and gifted teacher. In 1966, Priscilla earned a bachelor's degree in education.

*July 1968,*

*Priscilla with her two sons and daughter.*

# PRISCILLA JOYCE FORD

During this time, she married and had three children: two sons and a daughter. Her husband died in the late sixties. In 1970, shortly after his death, Priscilla's friends and family noticed that her behavior had started to become somewhat bizarre. She was reputed to talk about having seen her deceased husband opposite her house in Buffalo, New York and began talking about possessing the souls of Jesus Christ and Adam.

When her son returned from Army duty in 1972, he was shocked to find his mother an alcoholic and delusional. In 1973, Priscilla moved to Reno, Nevada and voluntarily committed herself to the Mental Health Hospital of Nevada. Here, she was diagnosed with a passive-aggressive personality disorder accompanied by hysterical episodes. She was prescribed medication and released.

In 1974, Priscilla was found trespassing and arrested. The court ordered a mental health evaluation. Priscilla's eleven-year-old daughter, Wynter Scott, was taken into foster care. Priscilla became most distressed about this and considered Wynter to be a victim of kidnapping.

Following the loss of her daughter, Priscilla drifted from place to place. For a while, she returned to Buffalo, New York and sought help from various charities to help her get her daughter back. In 1979, Priscilla became a patient at a mental health institute in Buffalo and was diagnosed with paranoid schizophrenia.

Upon her release, she moved to Maine. Here, in May of

1980, she sought the help of a lawyer. Priscilla wanted his help in regaining custody of her daughter Wynter. She reputedly told the attorney that if she wasn't helped, she would "drive across the state and kill every body she saw along the way." She also wrote many letters in her attempt to be reunited with her daughter. Priscilla, who neglected to take her prescribed medication for her schizophrenia, suspected evil beings were plotting against her.

By the time Priscilla moved back to Reno in November of 1980, she had been treated and released by seven different mental hospitals. Back in Reno, she secured herself a job at Macy's Department Store and found a small rental apartment to live in near Meadowood Mall.

On Thanksgiving-Day, November the 27th of 1980, Priscilla sat in her apartment munching cheese and crackers and drinking Emerald Dry White Wine.

In downtown Reno, it was a warm afternoon and maybe due to the pleasant weather, there were more tourists than normal strolling around casino row. The sound of music from passing car radios permeated through the air, competing with the street sounds of the mechanical ringing, clinking, and jingling slot machines.

The aroma of Thanksgiving special menus drifted through the streets as a sandwich board man, advertising a strip club, ambled slowly down the sidewalk.

Around 2.40 p.m., fifty-one year old Priscilla left her

apartment and climbed into her six-year-old blue Lincoln Continental and headed downtown. At approximately a hundred feet south of the southeast corner of Virginia and Second streets, Priscilla's Lincoln jumped the curb at a speed of about twenty miles an hour and moved rapidly along the sidewalk at a speed of about forty miles an hour, immediately killing five people.

The Blue Lincoln then crossed the Second Street crosswalk and continued on down the sidewalk for another 322 feet and then onto Virginia Street, where it crossed to the southbound lane and halted two blocks later, stuck behind traffic at a red traffic light on Fifth Street.

The carnage of body parts, ripped clothing, street signs, injured, and dead lying in the gutter and on the sidewalk resembled a war zone. It took only a couple of minutes for Priscilla to drive the five blocks but in that time, she killed five people and seriously injured twenty-four.

A woman tourist from Canada, who'd watched the event from her hotel, told the local Reno Evening Gazette,

"It looked as though someone had gone through the streets with a lawnmower, mowing people down. It looked like a battlefield—there were bodies all over the place."

Another witness stated,

"She came right at us. She came right at us with a woman's

body still on the hood of the car, and she looked like she was looking for somebody else to hit."

Ambulances and police officers descended on the scene, the injured were rushed to hospitals, and bodies were removed from the streets. Two more people died from their injuries after being taken to the hospital. Several dismembered limbs remained on the streets, along with upset trash cans, items that people had been carrying, and knocked over street signs. The casinos remained open. The affair was later referred to as the "Thanksgiving Day Massacre."

*Priscilla's carnage, 1980.*

# PRISCILLA JOYCE FORD

The police descended on the blue Lincoln Continental and removed 5-feet-4-inches-tall Priscilla from her car and arrested her. According to reports, she was angry that she had been stopped.

She was immediately taken to the Washoe Medical Center to determine her blood alcohol level — it was 162 — well over the legally prescribed limit.

John Oakes, the deputy district attorney, sat with Priscilla at the hospital. He later said that what was remarkable about her was her calmness, mixed with callousness. He reportedly said:

"She looked at me point-blank and said, 'How many people did I kill?' I said, 'Five or six.' She said, 'Good, the more dead beasts and pigs the better. I deliberately planned to get as many as possible. A Lincoln Continental can do a lot of damage, can't it?'

# FEMALE RAMPAGE KILLERS

*Priscilla's Car*

In December of 1980, Priscilla was indicted on six counts of murder and twenty-three counts of attempted murder.

On January 29, 1981, a judge found Priscilla incompetent to stand trial and ordered that she receive mental health treatment at Lake's Crossing so that she would be competent for trial. While receiving treatment, she allegedly told a psychiatrist that child welfare officials in Reno had kidnapped Wynter Scott, her eleven-year-old daughter, seven years previously and so she had committed the slaughter to get attention and receive help in finding her daughter.

In August of 1981, Priscilla pled not guilty due to insanity. On April 29, 1981, she was ordered to submit to treatment, including drug therapy. Finally, on August 4th, 1981, Priscilla was found competent for trial.

During the months before the trial, and during the actual trial itself, the expert medical witnesses testified that Priscilla was suffering from various mental illnesses—which included paranoid schizophrenia, paranoid psychosis, and religious delusions.

## TRIAL

The trial began on November 12th, 1981, and lasted nearly five months—which made it, at that time in Reno history, the longest

# PRISCILLA JOYCE FORD

and most expensive trial ever. Cal Dunlap, the District Attorney, was calling for the death penalty. Priscilla's attorney Lew Carnahan, a Public Defender, fought for not guilty due to insanity. The biggest argument during the long trial was whether Priscilla was aware that it was wrong to hurt and kill the people she had mowed down in her car.

Hundreds of witnesses testified including Priscilla's daughter, Wynter Scott. Wynter testified that her mother had taught her how to smoke marijuana at the age of nine and had talked to her about having her artificially inseminated in order for her to give birth to a messiah, by having a virgin birth.

During the course of the trial, Priscilla was judged competent and then incompetent to stand trial nor could she understand the charges against her. The prosecution argued that her prescription medicine made her competent, and the judge agreed.

Against her lawyer's advice, Priscilla testified in her own defense. During five days on the witness stand, she claimed she was the spirit of Jesus Christ, the Holy Spirit, and Adam reincarnate. She also testified,

"I am human, and I am divine. I do not like it any more than anyone else does. I don't want to be divine."

On March 20th, 1982 the five-men, seven-women jury took just thirteen hours to find Priscilla guilty of the murder of six people and the attempted murder of twenty-three others. They recommended the death penalty.

On March 29, 1982, Priscilla was sentenced to death in Nevada's gas chamber. Priscilla showed no emotion when the verdict was read.

Over the next eighteen years, Priscilla's lawyers launched a copious amount of appeals as she sat on death row in Ely, Nevada. They all failed. Nevertheless, Priscilla remained alive until January 1975 when, at the age of seventy-five, she died in prison from emphysema.

# SYLVIA WYNANDA SEEGRIST

## EARLY DAYS

Sylvia Seegrist was born on July 31$^{st}$, 1960 to middle-class academic parents Don and Ruth Seegrist in the port city of Oakland, in San Francisco Bay California. Sylvia was a bright, brown-eyed little girl who, by the age of four, knew the alphabet, could write her name, and seemed to have a life "full of promise." As an only child, her parents doted upon her. Her father lovingly built her a playhouse in the backyard, next to her swing. Sylvia, as a young child, enjoyed playing with the other children in the neighborhood, playing games, riding her tricycle or bike, and adored animals.

At the age of eight, the Seegrist family relocated to Springfield, Pennsylvania, a suburb of Philadelphia, located about 10 miles west of the city. Here, Sylvia's parents enrolled her in after school activities of acrobatics, guitar, horseback riding, and piano lessons, all of which she enjoyed.

During a visit during a summer vacation in 1973 to her

paternal grandparent's home in Virginia, Ruth overheard her mother-in-law harshly reprimanding Sylvia in a room upstairs and heard her thirteen-year-old daughter run to her room crying. Ruth immediately went upstairs and asked Sylvia what was wrong. Sylvia replied in between her sobs that her grandmother had shouted at her for saying her grandpa was not normal. Sylvia had then said,

"But mum, you just don't understand how intimate our relationship was."

Upon more questioning, Ruth learned that Ted Seegrist, Sylvia's grandfather, had masturbated in front of her and demonstrated to her the position for sexual intercourse when Sylvia had asked him "how babies were made," down "at their special place near the South River."

Ruth Seegrist testified years later in court that she had confronted her mother-in-law who'd,

"Slammed her hands over her ears and said, 'Don't tell me another word! Don't tell me another word! I don't want to hear it!"

Ruth and Don were not sure if Sylvia was telling the truth or maybe exaggerating but either way, it was a terrible shock. Ruth assured her daughter that she would ensure that Sylvia would never again spend time alone with her grandfather. She suggested that in future family visits to the grandparents that Sylvia remain "cordial and polite" towards her grandfather.

# SYLVIA WYNANDA SEEGRIST

Don and Ruth thought about getting a therapist for Sylvia at this time. But, once back at school after the vacation, Sylvia seemed to have forgotten the incident and was excelling at school, especially in math, science, and sports such as field hockey. Sylvia's ambition was to become a medical doctor. She had, as was normal with girls in their early teens, started to become clothes-conscious.

In 1975, at the age of fifteen, Sylvia began to show signs of rebelliousness: smoking marijuana and staying out all night. She became overtly disapproving of her mother, criticizing her taste in clothes, furniture, and even her hairdo. During a row with her parents, she told them she had been having sex since she was eleven years old. Ruth Seegrist said,

"She showed no shame."

At the time, her parents mistakenly thought that what she needed was "a good spanking." They had never hit her before. After her spanking, she was told she was grounded and sent to her room.

Later that night, Sylvia climbed out of her bedroom-window and told authorities that her parents had abused her. Her parents sent her to a therapist.

In March of 1976, while in class at school, she removed her shoes and began cursing as she paced round and round the classroom. An ambulance was called, and she was removed to the Institute of Pennsylvania Hospital where she was diagnosed as a schizophrenic. She was released into her parents' care in May of

1976.

Upon her release, her parents sent her to a private girls' school. All went well until, during a midterm exam in March of 1977, Sylvia drew pictures instead of answering the set of questions and fell into a catatonic state. She was once again admitted into the Institute of Pennsylvania Hospital but checked herself out on April 17$^{th}$, 1977. Sylvia was recommitted again on April the 29$^{th}$ and released into her parents' care in June of 1977.

That summer, Don and Ruth, feeling that Sylvia was slightly more stable, took a family vacation to Europe. While in Holland, Sylvia became depressed, spoke of killing herself, and swallowed a bottle of pills.

Back home in Springfield on October 1$^{st}$, Sylvia, after a row with her mother, repeatedly hit her. Her parents had her committed to the Haverford State Mental Hospital outside of Philadelphia.

This nightmare pattern was to continue repeatedly during the next eight years for Sylvia's parents. Many times, Sylvia would be released from the hospital before having been completely stabilized.

In 1978, Ruth managed to get Sylvia into the private University of Eastern College in St. David's. She was expelled after having been discovered to have had sex with seven male students.

Given the assaults on Ruth, the parents no longer felt safe having Sylvia live at home. However, they helped with her rent,

# SYLVIA WYNANDA SEEGRIST

drove her to work, and made sure she kept her appointments with counselors.

On May the 19th, 1980 during a counseling session, Sylvia threw a lighted cigarette into her counselor's face. The counselor had her committed involuntarily to Hahnemann Hospital: a mental health facility in Philadelphia. She was released on August 2nd of 1980 to Lansdowne Rehabilitation Center. Here, Sylvia stabbed a counselor with a fruit knife. This time, a court committed her to Haverford State Mental Hospital for six months. She was released in February of 1981.

On April 19th of 1982, her parents, having discovered that Sylvia had shaved her head bare, had her committed to Fitzgerald Mercy Crisis Center. She was released on May 10th, 1982.

On November 17th of 1982, Sylvia once again attacked her mother and yet again was committed to Haverford State Mental Hospital. In Sylvia's apartment, her parents found that she had taped all the window shades down, and her father discovered a handgun in a drawer. Her parents later asked her why she had a gun, and Sylvia told them that she was contemplating suicide but before doing so, she would kill them. Her parents turned the gun into the police. Sylvia was released from Haverford State Mental Hospital in early December of 1982.

In January of 1983, Sylvia was committed to a mental institute after having been found spray-painting her body with

## FEMALE RAMPAGE KILLERS

Swastikas and spraying on her apartment walls, "Kill them all," and "Kill, kill, kill." On March the 1st, 1983 she was released.

In December of 1983, Sylvia enlisted into the U.S. Army basic training camp at Fort Jackson, South Carolina. She was discharged two months later having being found unfit psychologically. Sylvia did not take the discharge well. For reasons unknown, she identified strongly with military might and the forces of war.

In July of 1984, the Springfield police arrested Sylvia for spraying hate graffiti in a public place. She was fined but refused to pay it and so was sentenced to Delaware County Prison for seven days.

On August the 3rd, Sylvia once again beat her mother and was committed involuntarily to the Sacred Heart Hospital but was released on August the 23rd. Upon her release, her parents bought her a car, a Datsun B-210, in an attempt to help make her more independent so she could drive herself to her therapy sessions. At the automobile license agency, Sylvia tried to strangle her mother and security guards intervened. Sylvia was recommitted on November the 9th for another three weeks. The hospital, despite offering a poor prognosis on Sylvia's mental health, could hold her no longer. They had to let her go by state law.

The Christmas of 1984, the family traveled to Virginia to spend the holiday with the paternal grandparents. During the entire vacation, Sylvia was agitated, restless, and continuously chain-smoked. On returning to Springfield, her parents persuaded Sylvia to take a correspondence course at Delaware County Community College. She dropped out midterm.

Sylvia then began dressing in military fatigues. Her frantic parents, realizing their daughter was dangerous, searched desperately for a residential program where she could get proper long-term treatment. They lived in fear that a terrible tragedy would occur, as Sylvia would frequently make threats such as,

"Someday, before I kill myself, I'll bring some people down with me."

Among Ruth's work colleagues, it was no secret she had problems with her daughter. Ruth spent much time and effort writing about her attempts to get her daughter institutionalized, hoping to spur local politicians to some kind of action. It didn't happen.

During the 1970s, the civil rights movement on behalf of the mentally ill had ensured that the mentally ill could not be institutionalized without a violent incident even if they needed hospitalization. In addition, once they were restored to calmer behavior, they were to be released.

Sylvia's main problem, apart from obviously being schizophrenic, was that she hated the side effects of her medication which included, among other things, loss of muscle control, weight gain, and problems with her sight; a problem common to many mentally ill patients, who frequently stop taking their medications for similar reasons.

In March of 1985, Sylvia attempted to buy a Ruger semiautomatic .22 caliber rifle at a local K-Mart. Store employees, seeing how she was dressed, sensed something was wrong. They took her deposit but when she returned to the store they lied and told her they had not been able to procure one. She took her deposit and left. The store manager later told reporters that she looked, "like she was ready to go into battle."

One wonders why they didn't report the incident to the authorities then.

Sylvia, a week later, went to Best Products and purchased a rifle for $104 after filling out a form saying that said she had no history of mental illness (which, by law, they were not required to check). Her parents and therapists were obviously unaware of this.

In the autumn of 1985, Ruth, tearing her hair out about her daughter, tried to persuade Sylvia to take some art classes thinking it might be therapeutic for her and promised to take her for a Thanksgiving vacation if she promised to stop wearing her military fatigues that she had now been wearing for months.

According to Jean Dolc, Sylvia's psychotherapist at the time, it had become a real cause of disagreement between Ruth and her daughter. During a therapy session, Sylvia had shouted at her mother, "Get off my back, you bitch," when the issue had come up.

# SYLVIA WYNANDA SEEGRIST

During September and October of 1985, Sylvia told her mother and Jean Dole that intense colors kept jumping out at her; she began wearing dark sunglasses and again taped her window blinds down. She talked about dreaming of mushroom clouds and being shot at in foxholes.

Don and Ruth were growing frantic. Sylvia was getting worse by the day both in her symptoms and in her anger. It was obvious to them that she needed to be in a secure mental facility. There appeared to be nowhere to turn to for help.

The local community was long familiar with Sylvia's eccentric character. Sometimes in September and October of 1985, she would be spotted in the local library in her army fatigues and beret mumbling to herself and, with the aid of a Russian dictionary, trying endlessly to translate books about bombs into Russian. Other times during this period, she would turn up at the local health club, fully dressed in her battle gear, to work out. One time, she sat fully dressed in the spa. An instructor at the club later said, "She hated everyone and would often talk about shooting and killing people."

Out on the street she would preach angrily from Muslim political propaganda. To anyone who would talk to her, she would say that she wanted to fight as a guerrilla in Iran. She would talk widely about "negative energy," a phenomenon that she was unable to explain to anyone who asked as her thinking was entirely disorganized.

## FEMALE RAMPAGE KILLERS

On October the 23rd, Sylvia marched up and down outside the entrance to the Springfield mall dressed in a red Arab-style headdress, wrap-around sunglasses, camouflage pants, and a T-shirt lettered with the phrase "Kill Them All."

On October the 27th, Sylvia visited the Chester County gun range and practiced target shooting.

At 4 a.m. on October the 29th, Sylvia telephoned and woke up her therapist, Jean Dole. According to Jean, she sounded more agitated and desperate than she had ever heard her sound before. Sylvia said to her,

"Get my mother to take me on vacation. I need a vacation."

In the morning, Jean telephoned Sylvia's mother Ruth. The two women agreed that Sylvia urgently needed persuading to commit herself. Later that day, when Ruth saw her daughter, Sylvia shoved a checkbook in her mother's face and grazed her cheek. Ruth threatened to have her committed involuntarily. Sylvia angrily left and went to a lawyer's office and wrote out a will.

The following morning on October 30th, Sylvia phoned her mother sounding better. Ruth felt a short-lived sense of relief but then Sylvia began "rambling about nuclear war, negative energy, and the end of the post office." Ruth begged Sylvia to commit herself which made Sylvia fly into a furious rage and shout at her mother,

"You fucking bitch! You have no right to interfere with my

life. I'm independent. Don't you ever talk to me again about medication and hospitalization. I would rather go to prison than back to the hospital."

Following this conversation with her mother, Sylvia made her way to the gym and worked out for half an hour dressed in her combat gear and gave the impression to the other people present of being extremely angry. She then made her way to the library and asked the librarian how many books she could take out once but failed to take any and left. She then went into a store and bought a few Halloween items. The shopkeeper remembered her well, as she had felt frightened by her hostility and aura of aggression. She then left the mall and returned to her apartment.

### THE RAMPAGE

Sylvia, at the age of just twenty-five, returned to the Springfield Mall wearing her red Arab-style headdress, wrap-around sunglasses, camouflage pants, and a Jihad T-shirt armed and ready. She parked her white Datsun car in the parking lot and retrieved her weapon from the back seat. Standing by her car she shot at a man, Edward Seitz, approximately thirty yards from where she stood. She missed and strode on purposefully to the entrance to the mall. On seeing a woman using an ATM machine, she took aim and again missed. She then spotted two-year-old Recife Cosmen standing in line with his parents outside a local restaurant. She fired, fatally wounding him in his lung and heart. Two other children standing near him were hit as well: a nine-year-old girl was shot in the right cheek and a ten-year-old received a minor superficial chest wound.

Once inside the shopping-mall Sylvia, muttering angrily, fired randomly into various stores. Many customers, upon hearing the gunshots, rapidly fled the mall. Ernest Trout was not so lucky. He was hit three times and dropped to the floor, critically wounded.

She shot and hit several more people, some of them were badly bleeding. Frequently, she missed and mostly people were only wounded. One woman was wounded in the back, another had two bullets in the abdomen, another girl had been shot twice in the stomach, and another young girl had a wounded hand. Outside Kinney's shoe shop, a 64-year-old man, Augusto Ferrara, stood looking at the shoes in the window seemingly oblivious to the carnage unfolding. Sylvia took aim and fatally wounded him. She then continued her march.

A young 24-year-old graduate student, John Laufer, watched Sylvia walk towards him. When she was about ten yards from him, she lifted her weapon to take aim. John moved quickly and took the weapon away with his right hand while grabbing her with his left. He said to her,

"You picked the wrong person to fool with this time. Now you're in a lot of trouble."

Sylvia apparently replied in a mumble,

# SYLVIA WYNANDA SEEGRIST

"I'm a woman, and I have family problems, and I have seizures."

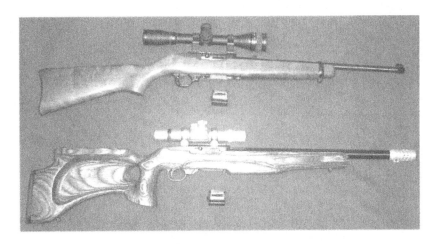

*Two Ruger 10/22 with rotary magazines; similar to the weapon used by Sylvia*

A security guard came to John's aid and handcuffed Sylvia asking,

"Why did you do this? Why did you shoot these people?"

"My family makes me nervous," replied Sylvia.

The police were notified and were on their way.

When they arrived and arrested her, Sylvia said to the arresting officers,

"Just shoot me now."

The rampage that had seemed to go on forever to those

affected in the shopping-mall had actually lasted only four- minutes.

The eight wounded and the two dead, two-year-old Recife Cosmen and 64-year-old Augusto Ferrara, were removed to hospital. The sixty-seven year old man, Ernest Trout, who had been shot three times, needed immediate surgery. One of the bullets had entered the frontal lobe of his brain and an eye.

Ernest Trout, who never regained consciousness, died on December 1st from a blood clot caused by the shooting. Even if he had survived, the prognosis was poor: blindness and paralysis.

That evening, an arraignment hearing was held for Sylvia before the District Justice in Springfield on two counts of murder, attempted murder, aggravated assault, possession of an instrument of crime, and carrying a gun without a license.

Sylvia was hauled into the courtroom, handcuffed and barefoot. Her first words to the Judge were,

"Fuck you. I hope you starve, motherfucker. I don't like that feeling, but that's the way it is."

The District justice ordered her to be held in jail without bail until the preliminary hearing, which was set for November 7th.

By the next day, the story of the rampage was in all the papers, most notably *The Philadelphia Inquirer* and on all the television stations.

# SYLVIA WYNANDA SEEGRIST

Ruth Seegrist gave an interview to reporters informing them that Sylvia had been diagnosed with schizophrenia at the age of fifteen and had been committed to psychiatric hospitals twelve separate times over the previous ten years.

At the preliminary hearing, it was argued by the defense that Sylvia was incompetent to stand trial. John Fong, a psychiatrist at Haverford State Hospital, stated that Sylvia was severely mentally disabled, and the staff at Mayview believed she needed continued involuntary treatment. Another preliminary hearing set for December the 6th was postponed.

Sylvia was transferred to Norristown State Hospital for evaluation by a court appointed psychiatrist, James Ewing.

On March 7, 1986, during a court hearing, Sylvia was declared competent to stand trial for the rampage with the proviso that before or during the trial, proceedings could be halted if her mental state deteriorated. Sylvia attended the hearing. She wore light purple slacks with a matching top and appeared well-groomed. Gone were the combat fatigues. She appeared subdued and frightened, like a scared little child.

## THE TRIAL

The trial finally opened on June the 18th, 1986. Sylvia was charged with three counts of murder, seven counts of attempted murder, and assault.

William Ryan Jr., the prosecutor, said the state believed that Sylvia had planned the attack and had committed it for attention. Sylvia's defense attorneys, Steven Leach and Ruth Schafer, argued that she was mentally ill and was unable to appreciate that what she was doing was wrong, that her thinking was delusional. They were heavily armed with testimony about her early sexual abuse, failures in the mental health system, and years of documented history of Sylvia's severe mental disability.

The prosecution paraded in front of the court witnesses who had been at the mall that day who testified about what they had seen and heard. The injuries to the victims were so graphically recounted that some people were in tears.

Prosecutor William Ryan Jr. argued that because Sylvia had done well in various psychology courses, she was well able to fool doctors. He brought Dr. Park Dietz to the stand who testified that Sylvia had known what she was doing was wrong. He said Sylvia had executed her rampage in an organized manner and had subsequently made statements to the police that indicated a planned attack under her control. He conclude that she was, therefore, not legally insane.

The defense introduced Ruth Seegrist to the stand. A dark-haired woman who resembled her daughter, she testified in a composed manner the years of suffering her and her husband had shared with their daughter's torment. Ruth described the bright, clever, and caring little girl who grew to become irrational, combative, and violent in her teen years.

Ruth drew tears from courtroom supporters who also had mentally ill family members when she described a conversation she had with Sylvia in April of 1985:

"Sylvia said to me, 'Mommy, don't you ever wish I were dead and not born? I have caused you and Daddy so much trouble, and I love you both so much. Now, tell me the truth,' she said. 'Don't you sometimes think how better off you'd be without me?'"

Ruth said she told her daughter,

"It's true sometimes in our darkest despair we have those thoughts, but they never last. Sometimes I wish you had cancer. At least then, you'd get treatment - compassionate, good treatment - and there wouldn't be the stigma connected with your illness."

The trial lasted eight days. At the end, the judge told the jury that they had four options: to find Sylvia guilty, not guilty, guilty but mentally ill, or not guilty by reason of insanity.

The jury of twelve took more than nine hours to deliver a verdict. Sylvia was found guilty but mentally ill.

The judge sentenced her to three consecutive life sentences, with a maximum of ten years each for the seven counts of attempted murder. He then ordered her to be sent to the Mayview State psychiatric Hospital for evaluation. Sylvia was eventually transferred to the State Correctional Institution at Muncy.

## AFTERMATH

The mental health system of Pennsylvania came under heavy criticism over the handling of Sylvia Seegrist's care over the years. For not only had there been several incidents of violence with her, there had only been minimal hospitalization, and there was no one professional psychiatrist to co-ordinate her care and treatment. More disturbing of all, two weeks before the Springfield shopping-mall incident, Sylvia had placed a call to a psychiatrist complaining of feeling agitated and anxious. The psychiatrist, rather than inviting her to attend a physical appointment, had simply given an over-the-phone prescription refill for a drug to calm her down.

Ruth's mother campaigned for legislators to make changes to the state mental health laws. Ruth said in an interview after another senseless killing case,

"You know, it's ironic that people who are irrational are expected under the law to get help on their own. There needs to be something in the law that compels a troubled person to be diagnosed by a psychiatrist. In the 1950s, we were institutionalizing people who weren't mentally ill. You could institutionalize someone who was just unruly. We've gone from one extreme to the other."

## SYLVIA WYNANDA SEEGRIST

In 1991, *Philadelphia Inquirer* journalist Reid Kanaley interviewed Sylvia. She said that with the help of treatment and new improved medication which she has received she no longer feels overwhelmed by anger, paranoia, or suffers from delusions. She said she hoped that one day she would be released. She continued to say that,

"Every time October 30 rolls around, I have a hard time that day. I have a hard time not crying. The idea that I hurt people; It's hard to describe."

She claims that at the time, she did not realize how sick she had been.

When Reid Kanaley asked her to explain her reasons for her actions, Sylvia said that she had been frightened that her mother was going to have her recommitted that day, and she so hated the medication she was on that she would have done anything to avoid that fate. She said she now hoped to earn a degree in psychology and eventually have a career in that field.

When the DA's office heard about her ambitions, they said they would strongly oppose her ever being released.

In 1994 the *Philadelphia Inquirer* did a follow-up piece which indicated that Sylvia had practically completed her psychology degree and was teaching math to fellow prisoners.

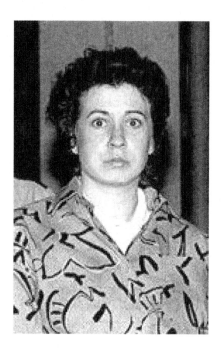

Now in 2013, Sylvia who is fifty-three, is a victim of a failed mental health system and sadly remains at the Muncy Prison.

Even more tragically, the mental Health system continues to let down those badly in need of help.

# LAFONDA FAY FOSTER and TINA HICKEY POWELL

### THE RAMPAGE

On a warm spring evening in Lexington, Kentucky, on April 23rd, 1986, two drug addicted young women, LaFonda Fay Foster, a twenty-two-year old prostitute and her lover, twenty-eight-year-old Tina Hickey Powell, had been on a four-day binge of cocaine and alcohol. They had now run out of money. Rather than call it a day, they set about obtaining some more money to buy yet more drugs and alcohol. Both women, although young, had spent time in prison over the years for fraud, narcotics, and robbery.

The two women made their way to an acquaintance's apartment, Virginia Kearns, at the Jennifer Road complex at around 4 p.m. When they arrived, Virginia, who was 45, lived with her semi-disabled husband Carlos who was 71 as well as her friend Trudy Harrell who was 59, was extremely drunk. The two women asked Virginia for money and said they weren't leaving until she gave them some. Virginia phoned the police and complained that two drunken women were in her apartment and would not leave. The police responded to the call and found Virginia drunk and the other two women appeared to the officers to be sober. The officers escorted LaFonda and Tina out of the apartment.

LaFonda and Tina made their way to a parking lot adjacent to the apartment block where a drinking party was in progress. The two women joined in, and Tina attempted to sell a knife to raise some money to buy another gram of cocaine. They then spotted Virginia Kearns walking towards a drug store. They followed her and a witness later said that they saw LaFonda shaking Virginia violently.

The three women then made their way back to Virginia's apartment. Virginia asked her husband to give the two women some money. At first, Carlos refused and an intense argument ensued. Carlos then agreed to write a $25.00 check but said they would have to drive to a fishing bait shop of a friend of his to cash it. Just then, two friends of the Kearns arrived at the flat: Theodore Sweet who was 53 and Roger Keene who was 47.

Under the direction of LaFonda and Tina, Virginia and Carlos Kearns, Trudy Harrell, Theodore Sweet, and Roger Keene all piled into the Kearns' car. LaFonda drove the car to the fishing bait shop where the manager cashed Carlos Kearns' check between 6:00 p.m. and 7:00 p.m. LaFonda then drove to the home of another acquaintance, Lester Luttrell, where the two women tried to get more

## LAFONDA FAY FOSTER and TINA POWELL

money. They failed, and LaFonda shot a .22 bullet into the window of his home.

The two women, with their five hostages, next drove to a deserted field off Mount Talbot Road. Here, they forced the hostages out of the car and told them to lie on the grass face down. Here, LaFonda shot Virginia and Carlos Kearns and Trudy Harrell, and Tina stabbed them. Although wounded, the three were ordered back into the car along with Theodore Sweet and Roger Keene.

LaFonda then drove to a nearby parking lot. Here, Trudy Harrell was hurled out of the car, stabbed a few more times, and had her throat slit. LaFonda then climbed back into the car and drove over Trudy's body. Her body became lodged under the car, and LaFonda needed to drive around and around the parking lot before it became dislodged. When the police discovered her body, there was no alcohol in her system.

Tina then drove the car to a bar about two miles away. A customer of the bar later testified in court that Tina had approached him and asked if he had any .22s or .38s bullets. He said he did not. Tina also asked the manager of the premises the same question explaining she needed to "shoot some rats." The manager handed over four .22 caliber bullets.

As LaFonda and Tina drove off, the manager noticed that the right passenger door had blood on it. He could not see who else was in the car but did notice a big guy with no shirt on. The women then drove to a loading area located behind a paint store. Here, LaFonda and Tina ordered Virginia out of the car.

A coroner later testified that Virginia Kearns had multiple stab wounds, sixteen of which were in her neck, her throat had been cut, and she had been shot in the head but despite her horrific injuries, what had killed her was being run over by a car and dragged along by the vehicle.

The two women then returned to the bar and asked for more bullets. The manager said he had no more. He also noticed that the blood he had seen previously on the car door had been wiped off. The two women and their remaining hostages then drove to LaFonda's father's trailer home where LaFonda went to get some ammunition from her father.

According to Tina's later testimony, while LaFonda was inside the trailer with her father, the three men begged her to help them. Tina claims she couldn't help them because LaFonda had taken the keys. When LaFonda returned to the car, they drove to a field off Richmond and Squires Roads. Here, the two women finished the last three hostages off. Each man was shot in the head, had their throats slashed, were stabbed repeatedly, and run over by the car. The two women then emptied a can of gasoline over the car and set it alight.

The two women then walked to the Humana Hospital on Richmond Road. While Tina called for a taxi, LaFonda went to a

## LAFONDA FAY FOSTER and TINA POWELL

bathroom to wash the blood off her face and hands. A nurse noticed the two women and the blood on their clothing and called the police. The police separately questioned the women. LaFonda and Tina claimed they had been in a fight with each other. The police noticed that both women stank of alcohol although neither had difficulty in walking or communicating. However, because the women were in a public place, the police decided to arrest them and take them to Fayette County Detention Center. At the detention center, three .22 caliber bullets were found on LaFonda and a blood-stained knife on Tina.

Once the bodies were found, it didn't take the police long to match the knife wounds to the knife found on Tina and to match the women's blood stained clothes to those of the five murdered victims.

*LaFonda and Tina Powell*

# FEMALE RAMPAGE KILLERS

## EARLY DAYS

LaFonda was born in Indiana in 1963. She began using drugs when only nine-years-old and attempted suicide three times at the ages of twelve, fourteen, and nineteen. Much of her childhood was spent being shuttled around amongst various relatives and foster homes. Consequently, her schooling suffered greatly, and she dropped out of school completely after the ninth grade. A male relative at one point sexually abused LaFonda and she supposedly had her feet burned when she objected.

LaFonda was first arrested at the age of thirteen for shoplifting and spent time in five different youth centers. Her first adult conviction for robbery resulted in a sentence of ten years, but she was released after serving one month and put on five years' probation. LaFonda had a long history of being beaten by men, being emotionally disturbed, and of having violent tendencies towards others.

Tina Powell was born in Youngstown, Ohio in 1958 but lived most of her life in Lexington. She left school before graduating and was married for a short time. She drank alcohol and took dugs frequently. By 1980, she had been arrested several times, mainly for drunkenness.

## TRIAL & SENTENCING

The two women went on trial together. LaFonda's defense team tried to show LaFonda as a victim of an abusive childhood,

## LAFONDA FAY FOSTER and TINA POWELL

battering, drugs, and violence. Tina's defense team used the strategy of blaming the events of the night on LaFonda by saying she was dominated, frightened, and in the total control of LaFonda.

After the four-week trial concluded, the jury recommended that Tina Powell be sentenced to life imprisonment without the benefit of parole and that LaFonda be sentenced to death on each of the five murder convictions.

The trial judge said that while he had sympathy for the abuse LaFonda had suffered as a child and as a young woman, he also had to consider other factors. He sentenced her to death making her the second woman ever sentenced to death in Kentucky. When he passed down his sentence, LaFonda bowed her head and cried.

Tina Powell was sentenced to life imprisonment without the possibility of parole for twenty-five years.

In 1991, LaFonda Fay Foster had her sentence overturned by the Kentucky Supreme Court. Prosecutors agreed to life without parole in 1999. LaFonda is serving her sentence at the Western Kentucky Correctional Complex in Lyon County, Fredonia.

Tina Powell had her first parole hearing in April of 2011. She told the parole board members that she didn't remember all that happened on the night of the murders because she and LaFonda had been using cocaine and drinking for about a week before the slayings. The parole board denied her parole. Tina Powell is serving her sentence at the Kentucky Correctional Institution for Women at

Pewee Valley.

*Tina Powell Mugshot*

According to the state Department of Corrections, Tina Powell and LaFonda Fay Foster have had numerous disciplinary violations while in prison.

# LAFONDA FAY FOSTER and TINA POWELL

### *Tina Powell aged 52*

The killings became the basis for a 1997 independent film, "100 Proof." LaFonda Fay Foster was also profiled and photographed in a book about people sentenced to death, *Final Exposure: Portraits from Death Row*.

# LAURIE DANN

Laurie Dann, née Wasserman, was born on October 18, 1957, the second child to accountant Norman Wasserman and his wife, Edith Joy. They were a Jewish family who then lived with their five-year-old son, Mark, in the Pill Hill neighborhood near South Shore, Chicago.

Seven years later, the Wasserman family moved to the affluent North Shore into a large, brick, tri-level home with big bay windows in Highland Park about 23 miles north of downtown Chicago. Laurie enjoyed a privileged upbringing. Laurie attended West Ridge Elementary School which was just four blocks from her home and Red Oak Junior High, where classmates remember her as always getting good grades. As a child, Laurie was shy and withdrawn.

"She was very, very quiet," a classmate said.

Laurie then attended Highland Park High School before transferring in 1973 to the elite New Trier East High School when the family moved to a larger house in the even more affluent area of Glencoe in northern Chicago on the west side of *Lake Michigan*. At school, Laurie found it hard to make girlfriends but because she was attractive, she was popular with the boys. Laurie graduated from New Trier High School in 1975. With not particularly good grades, she secured a place at Drake University in Des Moines, Iowa. While at Drake University, her grades improved, and she moved to the University of Arizona with the aim of becoming a teacher.

While at the University of Arizona, Laurie began dating a pre-med student, (who has since always wished to remain anonymous and for that reason I am giving him the name John Doe.) The relationship became serious, but John soon discovered that Laurie was too overly possessive and demanding. In 1980, after two years, the relationship ended, and Laurie moved back to her parents' home and transferred to Northwestern University to finish her degree. Laurie, though, dropped out of all of the courses she started and never graduated.

Laurie, for a while, took a job at Green Acres Country Club in Northbrook as a cocktail waitress. Here, she met Russell Dann the son of a wealthy Highland Park family. He worked for the family business Dann Brothers Insurance Co. in Northbrook. They started dating. Russell, like Laurie's father Norman, was a keen tennis player.

On vacation at Laurie's parents' Florida home in Boca Raton, the couple became engaged. They married when Laurie was 25 and Russell 26 on September the 11th, 1982 and bought a beautiful home for $275,000 at 367 Hastings Avenue in Highland Park. It was shortly after the marriage that Russell began to notice his new wife's strange behavior. What he had thought were cute quirks in Laurie's behavior when they were courting such as tiptoeing around a carpet at her parents' home and at stoplights opening the car door and tapping her foot on the pavement, he began to realize might be part of a much deeper problem.

Russell, thinking Laurie would be delighted with her beautiful new home, was disappointed to see that Laurie had zero interest in decorating her new home or even cleaning it. As the marriage progressed so it seemed did Laurie's problems. On the few occasions she did the laundry, she would fold it up dripping wet and put it away in drawers, leaving them to mold. She began to keep her makeup in the microwave. Kitchen cabinets were never closed, silverware only picked up with her sleeve or rubber gloves, and trash was strewn around the house. She began to compulsively scrub her hands. While her car, Russell's family thought, looked like the home of a bag lady but with cash thrown on the back seat like trash. With plenty of new clothes bought for her by her parents and Russell, she hung around in sweat suits and her dress became increasingly unkempt.

While Russell spent all day working hard at the office, Laurie spent her days watching television and became more and more reclusive. Russell finally persuaded her to see a psychiatrist, who diagnosed her as suffering from obsessive-compulsive disorder and identified her childhood and upbringing as a cause of her problems. But in March of 1984, Laurie refused to visit the psychiatrist any longer. A letter from her psychiatrist on March 12th pleaded with her to continue her psychotherapy.

"I am genuinely concerned about your ability to cope with the problems you have been struggling with."

The letter also warned Laurie that she could not rely on medication to cure her problems.

"The use of medication can only result in a symptomatic improvement and not in a definitive cure for the kinds of difficulties that you are experiencing. Medication can also only be appropriately administered under an ongoing doctor's observation and care."

By the autumn of 1985, Russell could no longer cope with Laurie's behavior, and the couple separated. Laurie moved back in with her parents', where her behavior became even more erratic and destructive as she continued her descent into an undiagnosed madness. Her parents handled her financial affairs and arranged for her to see several different doctors and therapists.

In August of 1986, she contacted her ex-boyfriend, John Doe, who was now a resident at a Tucson hospital in Arizona. She told him that she had given birth to his child. John refused to believe her. She then began harassing him with threatening phone calls. Laurie would call and say,

"I'm going to move out to Tucson and always be a part of your life."

The phone calls stopped only when John's lawyer sent Laurie's parents a letter requesting that they restrain their daughter.

Meanwhile, the divorce negotiations were exceedingly acrimonious, with Laurie claiming that Russell was abusive. Over the following months, the police were called to investigate various incidents. In April of 1986, Laurie accused Russell of breaking into and vandalizing her parents' house where she was then living. On May 10$^{th}$, 1986, Laurie purchased a .357 Smith & Wesson Magnum from a gun shop in Glenview. The store's clerk remembered Laurie as being pretty and flirtatious. Laurie told her parents that she needed the gun for protection, as she was frightened of Russell.

In August, Laurie began dating a close neighbor of her parents', John Childs. John's mother Alexandra Childs recalls that Laurie washed her hands frequently. John ended the relationship when he began to notice too many other idiosyncrasies.

In the autumn of 1986, while Russell Dann was asleep in his newly rented apartment in Highland Park, someone broke into his apartment and stabbed him with an icepick and punctured one of his lungs. Russell told police he did not see the intruder, but he strongly suspected it was Laurie. No charges were filed. However, a receipt for an ice pick was found in Laurie's home after the tragic events of May 1988.

# LAURIE DANN

After the stabbing incident, Russell and his family and friends began receiving late-night harassing phone calls. They were believed to be from Laurie. In November of 1986, Highland Park police arrested her for the harassing calls. The charges were later dropped due to lack of concrete evidence.

In January of 1987, Laurie decided to set herself up as a babysitter. She placed advertisements at a local convenience store, Dee Jay's Foods, and at the Glencoe library. One local mother, a trained social worker, used Laurie several times and recommended her to friends. Other families who employed Laurie as their babysitter would notice that their leather sofas had been slashed, their rugs cut up, and items would be missing. Other parents would notice that she would use pots, dishes, and cutlery and put them back in cabinets and drawers unwashed. One mother said,

"She had body odor like a longshoreman."

Others made complaints to the police about damage to their furniture and the theft of food and clothes. Despite the complaints, no charges were pressed as the evidence was circumstantial. Laurie would deny all knowledge of the damage or missing items. Laurie's father, Norman, did pay for damages in one case.

But nearly all the families that hired her, even those who suspected her of being a liar, thief, and vandalizer, said she was good with their children. The Bayless family, who had Laurie based on a recommendation by their next-door neighbors, Padraig and Marian

Rushe, were extremely happy with Laurie.

"Our daughter loved her," said Craig Bayless.

Just before Russell and Laurie's divorce was finalized on April 27$^{th}$ of 1987, Laurie accused Russell of raping her with a steak knife. There were no physical signs supporting Laurie's claim, although she passed two polygraph tests. No charges were filed. In May of 1987, Laurie accused Russell of placing an incendiary device in her parents' home. Again, no charges were filed.

By this time, Laurie was being treated by another psychiatrist for obsessive-compulsive disorder and a "chemical imbalance." The psychiatrist reported to police that he did not think Laurie was suicidal or homicidal.

During the summer of 1987, Laurie sublet a university apartment at 1725 Orrington Ave., from a student at Northwestern University on the Evanston campus. Again, her strange behavior was noted: wearing rubber gloves to touch metal and leaving meat to rot underneath the cushions of furniture. She soon became a suspect in thefts at the building and for several disruptive incidents, such as stuffing students' mail boxes with garbage. Other students complained of a stench from her room. The university inspected her room and found it to have urine-stained carpets and rancid meat on the counter. The North-western University authorities contacted her father, Norman, and said they needed to evict Laurie for turning her room into a health hazard. Laurie returned to her parents' home on

# LAURIE DANN

September the 7$^{th}$.

Back home, Laurie reverted to her telephone harassment of Russell Dann, his friends, and family.

"This was happening two or three times a night, five days in a row," said a friend who received calls.

A caller to the home of Susan Taylor, Russell's sister, said,

"Susie, Susie, Susie, you are going to die. Goodbye."

A local Glencoe detective, Floyd Mohr, was put on the case to investigate. In November, Laurie bought herself another gun, a .32 caliber Smith & Wesson and in December, she bought a 22 caliber semiautomatic Beretta. She was remembered in the shop as "just a friendly and pleasant person."

"There was absolutely nothing unusual about her," John Morgan, the owner of the shop said.

The phone calls to the ex-boyfriend in Tucson, Arizona also started up again but by 1988 these had now become death threats. The FBI was called in to investigate.

In January, Norman and Edith Joy Wasserman, her parents, persuaded Laurie to see a new psychiatrist, Dr. John Greist, a university psychiatrist in Madison, Wisconsin. To be near to him, Laurie moved into a campus room in a block known as The Towers. Here, Laurie told the other students that she was a sophomore studying journalism. It did not take long for the other students to notice Laurie's eccentric behavior. She became known as "psycho elevator lady" because of her habit of riding the elevator for endless stretches of the day and night, pushing buttons with her rubber gloves on and moving from floor to floor, but never exiting.

While in Madison, Laurie continued with her threatening calls to Russell, his friends, and his family, as well as to John in Tucson. Other people also began to receive death threats. One family that had hired Laurie as a baby-sitter and had accused her of stealing food and vandalizing their house received a death threat from a female caller.

"Your children are going to die."

In March of 1988, Laurie stopped attending her appointments with the psychiatrist and behavior therapist. Her psychiatrist and her father attempted to persuade her to enter a hospital as an inpatient, but she would not agree. On March 12, Laurie was reportedly seen in a laboratory at the University of Wisconsin Hospital. Three days later, a quantity of arsenic was found to be missing.

On March 14, Laurie was arrested at the J.C. Penney store in Madison and charged with shoplifting four wigs and two hairclips. She gave her address as the home she had once shared with her husband.

On May the 16$^{th}$, Laurie returned home to her parents' home in Glencoe, narrowly missing a visit from the F.B.I. in connection with the harassment phone calls.

# LAURIE DANN

## RAMPAGE

On the morning of May 20th, Laurie climbed into her mother's Toyota. On the back seat, she placed the three guns she had bought from the Marksmen gun shop and beside her on the front seat, she placed a bag full of little food packages and juices she had made, tainted with lead and arsenic. Laurie first drove to the Northwestern University in Evanston to two fraternity houses: the Alpha Tau Omega house and the Psi Upsilon house. Here, at 8 a.m., she left on their doorsteps paper plates piled high with Rice Krispy treats, marshmallows, and fruit drinks. Subsequently, seven students who ate the snacks were later treated at local hospitals for poisoning and released.

Laurie then went to the post office and mailed off a few of her food packages: one was sent to her husband Russell Dann and another to her psychiatrist, Dr. John Greist.

Laurie then delivered six more packages, leaving the packages on the front porches of family houses where she had baby-sat and who had made complaints about her.

Laurie then called in on the Rushes family and asked Mrs. Rush if she could take her two youngest children, Patrick, 6, and Carl, 4, out for a couple of hours. Mrs. Rush, who had always found Laurie good with her children, readily agreed.

## FEMALE RAMPAGE KILLERS

In the car, Laurie gave the boys two cartons of her special juice which, luckily, they didn't like. Laurie then drove to the Ravinia School in Highland Park where she believed her former sister-in-law, Susan Taylor's, children attended. Leaving the boys in the car, Laura started a small fire in the school hallway before running off and jumping back into the car. No one was hurt.

She then made her way to the Young Men's Jewish Council Day Center, attended by another of Susan Taylor's children, and walked up to the entrance carrying a can of gasoline, but she was prevented from entering.

Laurie then returned to the Rush's home. Here, she found Mrs. Rush in the basement doing the family laundry. Laurie left the children in the basement with their mother and made excuses to leave. As she made her way up the basement stairs, she lit a fire trapping Mrs. Rush and the two young children in the basement. Mrs. Rush managed to dislodge a small window and escaped with the children unharmed.

Laurie then drove to Hubbard Woods School at 1110 Chatfield Rd in Winnetka a school attended by Mrs. Rush's other children. Laurie entered Hubbard Woods School at about 10:30 a.m. She saw a six-year-old boy, Robert Trossman, standing by a water fountain; she dragged him into a nearby bathroom and shot him in the chest. Laurie then left him on the floor along with the weapon, a .357 Magnum pistol.

# LAURIE DANN

Amy Moses, a young, slight, petite, substitute teacher, was in her classroom at Hubbard Woods Elementary School having just settled twenty-four second-grade students down for a test on bicycle safety. When Laurie walked into the classroom dressed in baggy white shorts and a beige T-shirt bearing the image of a skeleton Amy had, at first, thought she was a student teacher come to watch the class. Laurie said to Amy,

"Put all of the children in the corner."

Amy, puzzled, said, "No."

Laurie then withdrew a pistol from her shorts. Amy put her hand on Laurie's arm and held the gun down. Laurie said,

"I have another one" and with that, Laurie withdrew another gun from her shorts, broke free from Amy, and began going up to each child and shooting them at point blank range. The children began screaming and running for cover.

Amy, saw someone outside in the school hallway and yelled,

"There's a woman in here with a gun."

Laurie then fled the school, leaving the traumatized young teacher to tend to the children as she waited for the police and ambulances to arrive. Amy Moses has never been able to teach again.

When the police arrived, they found the first of Laura's victims, the child in the bathroom. In the classroom, five more were wounded. Four of the children were in critical condition. One of them, Nick Corwin, 8-years-old, was pronounced dead on arrival at the hospital.

As news of the shooting spread through the neighborhood, terrified and anguished parents sped to the scene. Panic swept through the neighboring schools of the suburbs, as schools locked doors and barricaded windows with tables and desks. Students were ordered to stay in their classrooms and wait for their parents as fear that Laurie might target another school ran rampant through the area.

No one tried to stop Laurie as she left the school in her mother's car. She headed frantically down a dead end street and crashed into a tree. Abandoning the car, she grabbed her two remaining weapons and made her way into a wooded area. Here, she removed her shorts, spattered in blood from the shot children, and tied a garbage bag around her waist. Laurie then reloaded her .32 caliber Smith & Wesson revolver and .22 caliber Beretta before diving into a backyard and through an unlocked kitchen door of a house on Kent Road belonging to Raymond and Ruth Ann Andrews.

In the kitchen, Ruth Ann was chatting with her son Philip, a twenty-year-old University of Illinois student, when Laurie ran into the kitchen with a gun in either hand. She said she had just been raped. Andrew later recalled that she appeared highly distressed and agitated. She said she had shot her attacker and that now the police were after her.

Philip tried to calm her, and Ruth Ann offered Laurie a pair of her daughter's clean yellow shorts. While she was putting them on, Philip, unnoticed by Laurie, picked up the Beretta .22-caliber semiautomatic Beretta and removed the magazine.

At first, Ruth Ann and Philip were sympathetic and tried to convince Laurie that she need have no fear of the police since she had acted in self-defense. Raymond Andrews then joined the trio in the kitchen and tried to persuade Laurie to put down her weapon. Philip suggested that she call her family, and Laurie agreed and called her mother and told her that she had done something awful and that the police were involved.

"Mom," Laurie said. "I've done something terrible. People won't understand. I'm going to have to kill myself."

Her mother told her to turn herself in, that everything would be ok. Philip then took the phone and explained to Edith Wasserman about the rape and shooting and suggested that Edith should come to the house, but, according to Philip, Edith Wasserman said that she could not come as Laurie had her car.

"Can you take a cab?" Philip then asked. "Can you borrow a neighbor's car?"

Her response, he later said, was noncommittal. While Laurie and Philip were talking to Laurie's mother, Philip motioned to his parents to leave the house. This they did quietly and unobtrusively. Once outside, they alerted the police to what was going on in their house.

The police immediately assembled a swat team and surrounded the residence. Neighbouring homes in the quiet suburb were evacuated as heavily armed police teams took up positions around the house. The police brought with them to the house Laurie's parents and her ex-husband Russell Dann, hoping they could persuade her to give herself up.

Once alone with Laurie, Philip tried to disarm her. After a struggle, she shot him in the chest. The bullet punctured both of his lungs, severed his esophagus, ripped through his stomach and pancreas before lodging in the left side of his back. Philip struggled out of the house, collapsed on the driveway, and was taken immediately to the hospital for emergency surgery. He survived.

Laurie ran upstairs and barricaded herself in a child's bedroom. Laurie's father attempted to communicate with his daughter through a bullhorn.

"Please come out of there," he pleaded. "If you can hear me, please. Laurie, please come out."

The swat team entered the house at 7:23 p.m. and found Laurie, who had shot herself in the mouth, lying on her stomach with her eyes open…dead. When police told her father, Norman, he wept convulsively. The nine-hour ordeal was over.

Except it wasn't. There were too many unanswered

## LAURIE DANN

questions, severely wounded people, and traumatized families.

At Laurie's apartment in Madison, Wisconsin, the police found a list of people Laurie had delivered her packages to. On analysis, they all contained a heavy concentration of arsenic. They contacted all the people on the list to warn them.

Laurie left no suicide note explaining her actions.

### AFTERMATH

On a rainy day, young eight-year-old Nicky Corwin was buried. 1,500 family, friends, fellow pupils, parents, teachers, and neighbors attended the tearful farewell. On the same day, a few miles away, Laurie Dann was buried in a very quiet ceremony in a memorial park called Shalom.

Despite the severe injuries that some had received, all the wounded eventually recovered. The incident reawakened the debate about the criteria for committing mentally ill people to mental health facilities against their will.

For a young woman who had obviously been teetering on the edge for many years, why had the state of Illinois issued Laurie Dann a permit to buy firearms?

Why, with so many phone harassment threats, had Laurie not been apprehended?

Why had she never been hospitalized?

# FEMALE RAMPAGE KILLERS

Laurie Dann's psychiatrist, Dr. John Greist, in Wisconsin was stunned to learn after Laurie's May 20$^{th}$ shooting spree that she owned three guns and that she had been in trouble with the police; information he might have been able to use to build a case that she was dangerous and should be committed. Why had her parents not told him?

A local psychiatrist, familiar with the case, criticized her parents for shielding her from the consequences of her increasingly antisocial behavior. Laurie's parents, Norman and Edith Wasserman, were held liable to several lawsuits. A Cook County Circuit Court judge ruled that the victims of Laurie Dann's shooting spree could go ahead with lawsuits charging her parents with negligence. Judge Donald O'Connell ruled that Laurie's parents would have to defend themselves at trial against allegations that they knew their daughter was armed and dangerous and failed to get help for her.

Judge Donald O'Connell ruled,

"Under the allegations of this complaint, public policy considerations will not allow the defendants to be insulated from liability after engaging in the affirmative conduct to protect and control Dann, a person with known dangerous propensities and documented dangerous acts, and thereby disregarding the danger posed to society by virtue of their affirmative conduct."

The Wassermans' attorneys, Harry Wilson and Robert Reifenberg, had asked O'Connell to dismiss the suit on grounds that the parents were not present at the time of the shootings and because the shootings occurred away from the Wassermans' home.

But Judge Donald O'Connell ruled that,

"The public policy of the State of Illinois must recognize a cause of action against defendants who fail to act reasonably."

Albert Hofeld, one of the plaintiffs' attorneys, had argued that Laurie's parents had allowed her to accumulate weapons in their home and build bombs and were present at least part of the time. At the same time, they were telling a psychiatrist there was no evidence that she had a violent background and were falsely promising Glencoe police that they would take the weapons away from her.

"The parents were in control of their daughter, knew she was armed and dangerous, and failed to get her help," Hofeld said outside the court.

Norman and Edith Wasserman settled the lawsuits filed against them privately out of court. The Wassermans sold their Glencoe home shortly after the events of May 20th, 1988 and moved fulltime to their vacation home in Boca Raton, Florida.

Norman Wasserman's only public statement, written five days after Laurie's rampage, contains no hint that he accepts any responsibility or feels the need to offer any apology.

"Mrs. Wasserman and I reach out to all the families in their suffering. We suffer with you. Our prayer is that time will help alleviate the pain."

In the aftermath of the shootings, parents and members of the community devoted many years to gun control policy. Philip Andrew later became active in local and state gun control organizations; He subsequently became a lawyer and then an FBI agent.

# JILLIAN ROBBINS

Another case of a young girl not receiving the mental health care she needed is Jillian Robbins, who was born in 1977.

Jillian's parents separated when she was a young child, and she grew up with her mother in Pennsylvania but spent much time being bounced between parents. Her mother, Sirkka-Lila- Robbins, counseled international students at Penn State.

When Jillian was eleven, she told her mother she wanted to die. Her mother, realizing this was not a normal feeling for such a young child, took her to a counselor. The counseling continued throughout her childhood. Jillian later said that when she was a 10th grader, she heard voices and suffered from hallucinations where she saw "tall, dark people with dark coats and no eyes."

As a young teen Jillian, learned to ride and joined a swim team. She also won awards from the Red Cross and the State House of Representatives.

At 17, Jillian went to live with her father, David Robbins, an administrator with the Army Reserves in Dubois, a city 91 miles northeast of Pittsburgh. That year, still in high school, she signed up in March of 1994 with a reserve company in Bellefonte where she became a rifle expert. Jillian denied having suffered from any mental illness on the enlistment form.

David Robbins, her father, gave Jillian a high-powered 7-mm Mauser hunting rifle as a present. When giving it to her he said,

"Don't sell it and don't shoot anybody."

After completing a 10-week Army basic training, in June and July of 1994 Jillian dropped out of DuBois Area High School and checked into a mental hospital. One year later, the Army discharged her for not finishing high school. Jillian, in December of 1994, moved back with her mother and got a job at the state college diner. Here, she met Kenneth Walter Williams a fellow worker. They married on August the 1st, 1995, and rented a studio apartment from a woman named Kathryn Park but five months after the wedding, Jillian moved out of the apartment. Jillian found the marriage breakdown hard and checked into the Meadows Psychiatric Center, a private mental care facility on a spacious 52-acre rural campus located minutes away from State College in Central Pennsylvania.

Following her release from the hospital, she continued receiving treatment from a number of psychologists. One of them, Wilbur Wadlington, a State College psychologist, she began seeing in April of 1996. She claimed to have told him of her urges to "commit random acts of violence" and of owning the high-powered

7-mm Mauser hunting rifle. She was also seeing psychiatrist Katherine Thomson, who prescribed her medication which Jillian was reluctant to take because it made her feel drowsy and let loose "graphic, vivid nightmares."

In October of 1996, Jillian, after receiving her divorce papers, overdosed on tranquilizers. She was admitted to the Meadows Psychiatric Facility for a brief period and sent home with no medication.

On the cold, wet, dreary Tuesday morning of September 17th, 1996, Jillian awoke feeling more depressed than ever before. She felt like she could no longer handle the stress of her life, her hallucinations, or her delusions any longer.

Jillian left her Turtle Creek Apartment in Toftrees Avenue at around 7:45a.m. armed with nine rounds of ammunition, a 7mm Mauser rifle on her back hidden under a weatherproof poncho, and a knife. She began to walk towards the Penn state campus. On the way, she stopped at a convenience store where she bought a newspaper and a juice.

On reaching the campus grounds, she spread out a rain mat under some bushes near the Hetzel Union Building. Her intention was to shoot herself but before doing so, she read the newspaper and drank her juice.

Jillian years later said she then felt an explosion of "insane rage." With the loaded high-powered rifle in her hands, she began firing random shots at university students. The first shot hit and killed 21-year-old Melanie Spalla, a journalism major, 130 feet away from where Jillian was crouching. Another shot severely wounded 22-year-old Nicholas Mensah, a native of Ghana. Jillian continued firing shots. Two more ripped through backpacks containing books and preventing injury from the students carrying them.

Brendon Malovrh, 21, an aerospace engineering major heard the gunshots and identified where they were coming from. He crept up on Jillian and wrestled the rifle out of her hands. She then pulled a knife and went to stab him. Brendon stepped out of the way, and Jillian stabbed herself in the thigh which began to produce excessive blood loss. Brendon applied a tourniquet to her leg with his belt and waited with Jillian for the Penn State Police to arrive.

Jillian was arrested at the scene of the shootings and later charged with first-degree murder, attempted murder, and aggravated assault. She was nineteen-years-old.

During a preliminary hearing shortly after the incident, Jillian said,

"I don't know why. I just started shooting; I tried to reload, so I could shoot myself."

She was ordered to be held at Clinton County Prison to await trial. While there, the prison officials notified the court that Jillian needed mental health care. She was transferred to Norristown Psychiatric facility.

# JILLIAN ROBBINS

Acquaintances of Jillian Robbins admitted that she was known as crazy Jill. Others described her as energetic, friendly, flirtatious, and smart; While others have described her as sullen, aimless, unmotivated, and withdrawn. Employees where she worked over the 15 months prior to the shootings spoke of an artistic, witty, tomboy with a passion for exotic pets, funky hairstyles, and imported cigars.

Kathryn Park, who once rented an apartment to her, said;

"She's not the monster the media is making her out to be. She does need help, though."

*Jillian Robbins*

Jillian spent six months at the Norristown Psychiatric Facility before being sentenced to 30-to-60-years after pleading guilty to third-degree murder in 1998.

In a letter after the shooting rampage, Jillian requested her mother to sue the Meadows Psychiatric Facility for discharging her too soon and the State College Psychiatric practice because "[they] didn't listen when I told one of their monkeys I was going to kill people."

Today, Jillian is serving her sentence at the Women's State Correctional Facility in Muncy, PENNSYLVANIA.

It will not be until 2028 that Jillian will be eligible for parole.

# JENNIFER SAN MARCO

On January 30$^{th}$, 2006 on a warmish Monday evening in Goleta, a picturesque coastal city about 8 miles west of the city of Santa Barbara, forty-four-year-old Jennifer San Marco, an ex-resident of the city, drew up in her red pickup sometime between 7:15 and 8:15 p.m. outside the 5200 block of Overpass Road. She was calling uninvited and unannounced on her ex-neighbor Beverly Graham, who was fifty-four.

Three years previously, Jennifer had owned a condominium on the block. Her condo's back patio lay across a curving garden path to the front of Beverly Graham's where a Buddha statue sat by the front door, under a wind chime weighted down with Chinese coins. Jennifer disliked Beverly as she had repeatedly complained about Jennifer singing on her patio. After all, it was her condo, why could she not sing? Jennifer quietly went to the back of Beverly's condo, scaled the fence surrounding her back patio, and slipped into Beverly's home through an unlocked, sliding-glass door. Taking Beverly by surprise, she raised a 9-millimeter Smith & Wesson handgun and shot Beverly once through the head. Beverly immediately fell to the floor and puddles of blood began soaking through the beige carpeting of the blood-spattered walls of the hallway. A Nordstrom gift bag -- left over from a fifty-fourth birthday shopping expedition Beverly had undertaken the previous week -- sat on the stairs. Jennifer opened the front door and strode purposefully back to her car.

Jennifer then drove to a mail processing plant and distribution center at 400 Storke Road, Goleta where she had worked for six years. She had been dismissed two years previously and given a disability retirement in 2003 for unspecified psychological reasons. Jennifer arrived there shortly after 9:00 p.m. She entered the security gate by closely following a car in front of her. Parking her car in the worker's parking lot, she gained entry to the building by taking an employee's identification badge from a man at gunpoint. Jennifer then shot two people in the parking lot before gaining access to the building where she shot four more workers before turning the gun on herself and taking her own life.

Five people died at the mail processing plant from their wounds and the sixth person, Charlotte Colton, who was 44, died two days later in the hospital.

## JENNIFER SAN MARCO

It was the deadliest shooting at any workplace in the United States since 2003, when forty-eight-year-old Doug Williams gunned down fourteen co-workers at a Lockheed Martin aircraft parts plant in Meridian, Mississippi, killing six before turning the gun on himself.

## JENNIFER'S BACKGROUND

Jennifer San Marco was born on December 6th, 1961 in Brooklyn, New York and attended Brooklyn's Edward R. Murrow High School where she was enrolled in handball, the drawing club, and involved in business classes. Fellow classmates remember her as been very pretty and quiet.

Jennifer then went on to study at Brooklyn College before attending Rutgers University in New Jersey where she studied natural resources management but failed to graduate. In 1989, Jennifer moved to Goleta with the help of a cousin who lived in Montecito in Santa Barbara County, California. She rented an apartment from the landlord, Ms. Chandos Hoffman, who reported that in the fourteen months that Jennifer rented the apartment, not once did she have any visitors. Ms Chandos said Jennifer was very isolated, and she worried about her. She herself remembered Jennifer as being polite and friendly.

Jennifer had taken a job as a secretary at Canterbury Career School in Colton while attending a state corrections officer's academy. From there, she went on to work for the California

# FEMALE RAMPAGE KILLERS

Department of Corrections as a guard at Chuckawalla Valley State medium-security Prison in Blythe. She left this job two days prior to her probation period ending. A correction's officer at Chuckawalla, Lieutenant Steve Sapp, said, "She didn't tell us why." He also remembered her as being a "good officer."

*Jennifer San Marco*

Over the next several years, Jennifer held a number of jobs including being a Santa Barbara police dispatcher, a job for which she underwent a background check and psychological evaluation. But this job, according to Chandos Hoffman, "She found really hard and stressful."

In 1997, Jennifer began working nights at the Goleta mail sorting plant and bought a condominium at the 5200 block of Overpass Road. During 2002, Jennifer's workmates and neighbors

## JENNIFER SAN MARCO

began to notice a deterioration in Jennifer's behavior. According to a former neighbor, Jeannie Steen, Jennifer would scream profane rap lyrics and shout death threats. Jeannie said, "The passion of her anger was hard to describe. It was so frightening."

Frequently, Beverly Graham, before Jennifer murdered her, would tell her boyfriend, Eddie Blomfield, that she was going to call the police on her noisy neighbor, but her boyfriend advised against it.

"She's just nuts," Eddie would say.

"Jennifer was crazy," said Eddie Blomfield. "She'd stand outside and sing as loud as she could. She'd go on tirades and rant and rave. Beverly would open the door and tell her to shut up which led to arguments between the women."

Beverly's brother Les Graham Jr. said his sister frequently complained to him about Jennifer disturbing and upsetting her.

Jennifer's behavior at work became more erratic and upsetting to her fellow workers. Finally, in 2003, authorities at the postal facility called the police, and sheriff's deputies dragged her out from under a sorting machine and took her to a mental health facility in Ventura for three days of assessment. It's not known whether Jennifer received any therapy there or anywhere else.

Jennifer returned to work a couple of months later, but her co-workers found her acting erratically.

"She would scream and say a lot of racist comments. It was pretty ugly," said one former colleague of Jennifer's.

"She seemed to be having conversations, and there wasn't anyone around her. She'd be just jabbering away," said another former co-worker.

Finally, after many complaints from her colleagues, Jennifer was placed on involuntary medical leave from the Postal Service in June of 2003 and was escorted out of the building by management.

## NEW MEXICO

On losing her job, which Jennifer believed was a conspiracy against her by the postal department, Jennifer put her condominium up for sale and decided to move back to New York to be near her brother.

In 1994, driving back to New York along U.S. Route 66, her car broke down in Grants, New Mexico, a town that had achieved fame as the "carrot capital" of the United States as the area's volcanic soils provided ideal conditions for farming. While her car was being repaired, Jennifer decided she liked the tranquility of the area and decided to stay. She found a yellow two-story house on three acres of dusty hillside between the village of Milan and Grants.

John Phillip, an auto body shop owner, who repaired her car said she talked about the Postal Service having mistreated her.

"She never talked about anything violent, but she did say

things like 'I hope they pay.' She just never said anything about killing."

Jennifer quickly earned a reputation in both Milan and Grants as "the crazy lady." The locals would see her going through local Dumpsters, parking on the side of the road and praying, or talking and shouting furiously to herself. She was also known to order food at restaurants and bolt out the door before eating it, as well as someone who peeled off her clothes in random parking lots.

Nobody knew where she came from or what she was doing there. People just knew there was something wrong. She had no history on her, any family or friends, and was always by herself.

In July of 2004, she called into the Milan village offices, paying a $35 fee to sign up for a business license for "The Racist Press." A publication she tried to distribute that included error-laden explanations of various religions and a confusing theory linking the U.S. government to the Ku Klux Klan, "Son of Sam" killer David Berkowitz, and racist murders. Those who saw her that day in the office recalled that she sat mumbling to herself in a way that sounded as if she were two people arguing.

A few weeks later, she called into the offices again wanting to register a cat food business. However, both her applications were turned down as she lived in an unincorporated area of Cibola County.

Despite having both her applications turned down, it did not deter Jennifer from making frequent visits to the office. She became fixated on one particular female employee, Sonya Salazar.

"She would just come in here and stare at me," said Sonya. "We knew she had mental problems. We just felt sorry for her."

Other workers would warn Sonya when Jennifer was coming so she could hide.

"She would come in and just ask questions about area projects. Sometimes we weren't sure what she was referring to. A lot of times she would storm in, blurt out something, and walk out," said another worker.

But on one particular day, she strode into the offices and was so abusive to Sonya that the manager, Carlos Montoya, felt obliged to call the police and make a complaint of verbal harassment. The police were contacted about Jennifer on another occasion, in June 2005, when she appeared naked at a gas station in Grants.

"We stopped her on a complaint of nudity and warned her about state law. We basically told her not to be doing that and sent her on her way," police Chief Marty Vigil said.

Throughout 2005, the locals observed Jennifer becoming more and more unkempt.

"Her hair looked like, one time, she cut it with a hacksaw or something," said one local.

However, despite all this bizarre behavior, it did not prevent

## JENNIFER SAN MARCO

Jennifer from purchasing a lethal weapon. In August 2005 Jennifer visited the pawn shop, Ace Pawn and Antiques, in the city of Grants and purchased a 15-round, 9 mm Smith & Wesson model 915 for $325 and an unknown amount of ammunition from a pawn shop in Gallup, New Mexico. The owner of Ace Pawn and Antiques, Paul Castillo, said she filled out an application for a background check, which didn't turn up any problems, and picked up the gun two days later.

**WHY?**

After the rampage, the authorities searched Jennifer's home looking for clues as to why she had done what she had. The authorities found notebooks of different writings that alluded to a conspiracy involving workers at the Goleta mail-sorting plant against her. They also found a diary of more than 100 pages in length that contained meticulous notes of perceived slights and offenses she had received from people.

"She obviously felt that the post office was out to get her in one way or another. That establishes as good of a motive (for the killings) as we can determine at this point," said a spokesman for the Santa Barbara County Sheriff's Department.

Santa Barbara County Sheriff Jim Anderson said it wasn't clear if the killings were racially motivated. As Jennifer San Marco had left behind no suicide note, her motives remain in question.

Of her seven victims, three were black, one was Chinese-

## FEMALE RAMPAGE KILLERS

American, one was Filipino, and one was Hispanic. Only Beverly Graham was white. Killed were Beverly Graham, 54, Ze Fairchild, 37, Maleka Higgins, 28, Nicola Grant, 42, Guadalupe Swartz, 52, Dexter Shannon, 57, and Charlotte Colton, 44.

Criminologists called Jennifer San Marco's rampage the worst workplace shooting by a woman in United States history.

# AMY BISHOP

Amy Bishop was born on April 24, 1965 to Samuel and Judith Bishop in Braintree, Massachusetts. When she was three years old, her baby brother Seth was born. Amy's father was a Professor in the Art Department at Northeastern University in Boston. Her mother, Judith, was a keen equestrian and heavily involved in local politics.

At Braintree High School, Amy and Seth excelled at their studies, and Amy accepted a place to study Biology at Northeastern University, Boston. She was joined there three years later by Seth, an excellent violinist, who had enrolled in an engineering program.

Tragedy struck the family when, at the age of twenty-one, on December 6, 1986, during Christmas vacation at the Braintree family home, Amy shot her eighteen-year-old brother dead: A murder that was to lay hushed and covered up for over twenty-four years.

# FEMALE RAMPAGE KILLERS

The event, in which Amy fired at least three shots from a pump-action 12-gauge shotgun, was full of differing accounts. After firing the shots and killing her brother, she fled the house to a car dealership, where she pointed the loaded gun at employees and demanded a getaway car. She told them her husband was going to come after her, and she needed to flee.

Amy was eventually unarmed and taken into custody by the Braintree police. The police found the shotgun to be loaded, which was only possible if, after Amy had shot Seth, she racked the slide of the gun to simultaneously eject the spent shell and reload the chamber.

Amy could have been charged with assault with a dangerous weapon, carrying a dangerous weapon, and unlawful possession of ammunition, let alone murder or manslaughter. The then Braintree police chief, John Polio, a close friend of Judith Bishop, ordered Amy to be released to her mother.

A member of the police department remembered that at the time there were many officers who "were frustrated over the release." Other officers believed that John Polio had "fixed a murder," resulting in "a miscarriage of justice simply because of his friendship with Judith Bishop."

Amy and her parents testified during the inquest into Seth's death that it was a horrific accident, not a crime, according to transcripts of their testimony. Shortly after this, the files relating to

# AMY BISHOP

the shooting disappeared.

Amy returned to Northeastern University and graduated with a Bachelor of Science degree in biology in 1988. After graduating, she married her university sweetheart, fellow biologist James Anderson, at All Soul's Church where Seth's funeral had been held. The pair remained in Boston for a while, buying a home on Birch Lane in Ipswich on Massachusetts' North Shore. Here, they had four children. During this time, Amy took various positions in labs at Boston hospitals and in 1993 earned her Ph.D. in genetics from Harvard University.

Amy, in 1993, then worked at the Boston's Children's Hospital neurobiology lab. Her supervisor, Dr. Paul Rosenberg, a Harvard Medical School professor and physician at Children's Hospital Boston, gave Amy a negative evaluation of her work. He felt that she "could not meet the standards required for the work." Amy was extremely upset and resigned from her position at the hospital.

In December of 1994, Dr. Paul Rosenberg and his wife, on returning home after a Caribbean vacation to Newton, Mass, began opening the pile of mail that had accumulated during their absence, when Paul noticed in a parcel two cylinders wired to a 9-volt battery. Paul and his wife immediately departed the house for a neighbor's house and called the police. The police arrived and identified the device as a pipe bomb that had failed to detonate. Luckily, no one was harmed.

Amy and her husband James Anderson became suspects and were questioned. Amy and James provided handwriting samples as required but refused to submit to a polygraph test. Investigators confiscated Amy's notebooks and computer and discovered that Amy Bishop was working on a novel about a woman who killed her brother and then tried to redeem herself by becoming a successful scientist.

The pipe-bomb case was never solved due to lack of evidence.

While living in Ipswich, Amy was a member of the Hamilton Writing Club. According to a fellow member of the writing group, Amy had written three unpublished novels one of which featured a female scientist working to defeat a potential pandemic virus and struggling with suicidal thoughts at the threat of not earning tenure. She also boasted to the other members about being related to John Irving, *The Cider House Rules* author, who is her mother's cousin.

In 2002, Amy took her children to the International House of Pancakes in Peabody, Massachusetts, about halfway between their Ipswich home and Boston. She went to fetch a booster chair for her youngest child but missed the last one by minutes. Amy strode up to the woman, Michelle Gjika, who had taken the last one and demanded the seat while launching into a profanity-laced rant. When Michelle Gjika refused to give it to her, Amy punched her in the

# AMY BISHOP

head whilst yelling,

"Don't you know who I am? I am Dr. Amy Bishop."

The police were called. Amy pleaded guilty to two misdemeanors: assault and battery and disorderly conduct. She was sentenced to six months' probation and ordered to enroll in an anger management course. Her husband later said she had never attended the anger management classes.

In 2003, Amy was offered a position as a Professor in the Department of Biology at the University of Alabama in the city of Huntsville. Amy and James sold their Ipswich home and bought a house in Huntsville which is located in Madison County in the northernmost part of the U.S. state of Alabama and is the fourth largest city in Alabama. Nearby is NASA's Marshall Space Flight Center and the United States Army Aviation and Missile Command.

Amy hoped that she would be able to achieve tenure at the University of Alabama. For most academics, a tenured position is the goal. Tenure guarantees job stability, meaning that a college or university cannot fire a tenured professor without presenting evidence that the professor is incompetent or behaving unprofessionally. To become a tenured professor, the average probationary period is three years for community colleges and seven years at four-year colleges. This is a period of employment insecurity virtually unique among U.S. professions. People denied tenure at the end of this time lose their jobs; tenure is an "up-or-out" process. The most recent survey of American faculties shows that, in a typical year, about one in five probationary faculty members was denied tenure and lost his or her job.

Amy Bishop's track record at the University of Alabama in Huntsville was mixed. She published only six papers during her time at UAH, about half the number that a biologist seeking tenure would normally be expected to produce. Also during her time at UAH, other members of the faculty had found her difficult. And at a lecture she gave as part of her tenure evaluation, she failed to impress the tenure committee. It was also noted that graduate students regularly transferred out of her lab or were dismissed, while other students had signed a petition claiming she was an ineffective teacher.

Another professor who was part of Amy's tenure-review committee referred to her as "crazy." He later said,

"I said she was crazy multiple times, and I stand by that. The woman had a pattern of erratic behavior. She did things that weren't normal... she was out of touch with reality."

In March of 2009, Amy's application for tenure was turned down, and she was expected not to have her teaching contract renewed after March 2010. Amy appealed the decision to the University's administration. Beyond the ego and stress involved in the tenure fight, Amy may have also been worried about the family's finances. Her husband James was only working part time, and Amy

# AMY BISHOP

was the chief breadwinner.

In November of 2009, the University of Alabama denied Amy tenure appeal without reviewing the content of the tenure application itself. They determined that the process had been carried out according to policy. Amy would have to find herself, at the age of forty-five, a new job by March of 2010. Amy was vocal among colleagues and anyone else who would listen about her displeasure over being forced to seek work elsewhere.

On a chilly overcast day on the morning of February 12$^{th}$, 2010 Amy taught her Introduction to Anatomy and Neurosciences class. Some students later reported that she "seemed perfectly normal" while others said that she seemed to ramble and that she had seemed confused when they asked her whether they were expected to attend her class on President's Day.

Following the lecture, Amy returned home for a couple of hours. Her husband, James, dropped her off on campus again at around 3:00 p.m. Amy made her way to the Shelby Center for Science and Technology and entered Room 369, a small conference room on the third floor for a routine staff meeting of the Biology Department. Amy and her fellow twelve colleagues crowded around an oval table in the small room.

## RAMPAGE

Debra Moriarity, professor of Biochemistry and Dean of the University's graduate program, chaired the meeting. Later, she said that Amy Bishop sat quietly at the meeting for thirty or forty minutes during which discussions ran from a spring open house to plans for the following fall.

*Shelby Center for Science and Technology*

Suddenly, Amy stood up and whipped out a 9-mm. Ruger semiautomatic gun from her handbag and began shooting her colleagues. She started with the one closest to her, Maria Ragland Davis, who was killed instantly while still seated at the table. She then went down the row shooting her targets in the head execution style without saying a word. The ones who had not been shot yet dived under the table, desperate for cover. Debra Moriarity said she

# AMY BISHOP

tried to grab Amy's legs, but Amy stepped out of her grasp. Amy then pointed the gun at Debra but when she pulled the trigger, only a click was heard. The gun had either ran out of ammunition or jammed.

Debra, seeing her chance, approached Amy and asked her to stop. Debra and the other survivors then made a rush at Amy and pushed her out of the room before barricading themselves in. The entire episode had lasted less than a minute. Six people had been shot, three of them fatally. Amy Bishop then disposed of the gun in a bathroom and telephoned her husband to pick her up in the parking lot. The police arrested her before he arrived.

*The scene shortly after the shooting*

Shortly after her arrest, when asked about the deaths of her colleagues, Amy was quoted as saying,

# FEMALE RAMPAGE KILLERS

"It didn't happen. There's no way. They're still alive."

**Victims**

Three faculty members were killed; they were:

- Gopi Podila
- Maria Ragland
- Adriel D. Johnson, Sr.

Three others were injured; they were:

- Luis Rogelio Cruz-Vera, released from the hospital on 2/4/10
- Joseph G. Leahy, released from the hospital on 4/14/10
- Stephanie Monticciolo, released from hospital on 3/29/10

Amy was suspended without pay retroactively on the day of the attack and later, in a one-paragraph letter dated February 26, 2010, she was fired. Amy received a letter of termination from Jack Fix, Dean of the College of Sciences, which did not state a reason for doing so. Her termination was effective February 12, 2010: the day of the shooting.

# AMY BISHOP

Amy was charged with one count of capital murder and three counts of attempted murder. James Anderson secured her an attorney, and she was held without bail at the Madison County Alabama jail. According to Alabama law, Amy was eligible for either the death penalty or life in prison.

The police, during their investigation, believe that the shootings were committed out of anger at having her tenure denied. The investigating police also learned of the shooting of her brother nearly twenty-four years earlier. They decided the case needed to be re-examined.

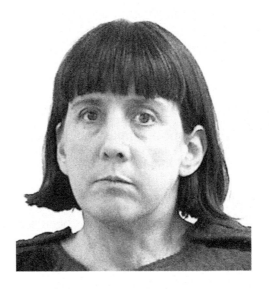

*Amy Bishop*

# FEMALE RAMPAGE KILLERS

The files about the case that in 1988 had disappeared were relocated and turned over to Norfolk County prosecutors following the shooting rampage at the University of Alabama. A grand jury indicted her on June 16th, 2010 on a charge of first-degree murder for the shooting of her brother, Seth Bishop.

William R. Keating, Norfolk District Attorney, announcing the indictment said law enforcement authorities in Massachusetts had failed to do their job properly in 1986.

"Jobs weren't done. Responsibilities weren't met. Justice wasn't served," William Keating said.

A conviction in 1986 might have changed Amy Bishop's life, potentially averting the Alabama tragedy, William Keating said.

"My heart goes out to them," he said of the Huntsville victims.

On June 18th, two days after Amy was indicted for the murder of her brother, she attempted suicide in jail. She survived and was treated at a hospital and then returned to jail.

James Anderson's father, Jim Anderson Sr., Amy's father in law, said that he, too, wished justice had been served back in 1986.

"We lost a talented young man, a violinist," he said, referring to Seth Bishop. "If justice had prevailed when he was shot and law enforcement had handled it correctly, Amy would have been able to either get criminally charged or get help, one or the other."

# AMY BISHOP

On September 11, 2012, Bishop pleaded guilty to the above charges in order to avoid the death penalty. The jury heard a condensed version of the evidence on September 24, 2012 as required by Alabama law. Amy Bishop was sentenced to life in prison without the possibility of parole on September 24, 2012.

In September of 2011, Amy pleaded not guilty by means of insanity. At that point, the prosecution were seeking the death penalty. In 2012, the spouse of one of the murdered victims wrote a letter to the judge presiding over the case. In this letter, the writer said that although the family had suffered greatly from their loss due to Amy's actions, they did not see any benefit from the loss of another life. The chief prosecutor, Robert Broussard, then contacted and learned from the nine survivors that none of them wanted the death sentence for Amy Bishop. Based on this, the prosecution contacted the defense team and said that if Amy pled guilty, the prosecution would not pursue the death penalty.

Amy changed her plea from not guilty by insanity to guilty and thus avoided the death penalty. On September 24, 2012, Amy Bishop, now forty-seven, was sentenced to life in prison without parole. In court, she was dressed in a red jail uniform and shackled at the feet.

Amy is serving her sentence at the Julia Tutwiler Prison for Women in Wetumpka, Alabama: a prison where a nonprofit group says there is widespread sexual abuse of the prisoners. In a 2007

Justice Department report, it was found that Tutwiler maintained the highest rate of sexual assault among prisons for women.

Given her sentence in Alabama, officials in Massachusetts said they would not be pursuing extraditing Amy to Massachusetts for the murder of her bother, Seth. The indictment was withdrawn without prejudice, which means it can be reinstated at any time. Amy, however, made a statement through her Massachusetts attorney, Larry Tipton, that she wants to be tried for her brother's death in order to vindicate herself and show that she had a "loving and caring relationship" with her brother Seth.

When Amy's husband was asked about the unpublished novel that Amy had supposedly written about a woman who had killed her brother and was hoping to make amends by becoming a great scientist, James Anderson said the novel was not autobiographical.

"It was just a novel. A medical thriller is the best way to describe it," he said.

On February 11th, 2013, Amy, after pleading guilty in September 2012 and waiving her right to appeal, filed an appeal. In the appeal, she stated that she had not been informed of the rights she would be waiving by pleading guilty, nor was she correctly informed of the minimum range of punishment, and the Circuit Court had failed to explain that she could withdraw her plea. On the 26th of April, 2013 the Alabama Court of Criminal Appeals rejected

Amy's appeal stating that Amy had failed to challenge the validity of her guilty pleas in the Circuit Court and had not filed either a motion to withdraw her pleas or a motion for a new trial.

Amy Bishop remains incarcerated at the Julia Tutwiler Prison.

# SABINE RADMACHER

In 2010, in the small town of Lörrach, Germany close to the French and Swiss borders, and a town twinned with Chester in the UK, residents were reeling in shock. On September 19, 2010 a 41-year-old woman, Sabine Radmacher suffocated her 5-year-old by first knocking him unconscious and then putting a bag on his head.

When her estranged husband, a 44-year-old carpenter, arrived at her apartment to collect his son, she shot him twice, once in the head and once in the neck before stabbing him. Sabine then set fire to the apartment with highly flammable nitrocellulose paint thinner, which eventually led to the flat exploding causing seventeen people to be injured by smoke inhalation. It is amazing that there were no worse injuries given the damage that occurred to the building.

*Sabine's estranged husband*

Once she had set the fire, Sabine made her way down to the street, clutching a 22-calibre sports pistol and a knife. Sabine then crossed the road over to St. Elizabethan Hospital.

Upon entering the hospital grounds, she opened fire on passersby, injuring two.

A nurse at the hospital, Sister Xaveria, said, "I heard shots and looked out of the window. This woman was running towards the entrance. She had a gun. I immediately grabbed the phone and called the emergency services. When she entered the clinic, she seemed quite calm. I saw her loading her gun and then she pointed at me. All I could do was duck under the table and remained there until the police arrived."

Sabine then made her way to the Gynecology Ward, here she shot and stabbed dead a 56-year-old male nurse, who was married with three children. She also severely injured two visitors and a police officer who happened to be visiting.

The police arrived, and Sabine opened fire at the officers. Police marksmen shot Sabine in a hail of bullets seventeen times until they were sure she was dead. The entire incident from the explosion to Sabine's death lasted 40 minutes. Afterwards, over 100 rounds of ammunition were found at the hospital. Sabine had been treated at the hospital in 2004 for a miscarriage, but no one knows if that was the reason why she started shooting in the hospital.

In fact, no one is entirely sure what triggered Sabine's murderous rampage. Sabine was a lawyer, and her work colleagues and friends said she had become increasingly distressed and resentful about the collapse of her relationship and a child custody dispute.

The couple were said to have separated in June and that the husband had custody of the son, who visited Sabine at weekends. Neighbors thought the husband had a new partner that had seemed to upset Sabine greatly.

# SABINE RADMACHER

*Sabine and son in happier days*

An unnamed neighbor told the German *Bild* newspaper: "She seems not to have got over the fact that the son lived with the father. She had lost everything: her husband, her child and her home. But I would never have thought she was capable of something like this."

# CONCLUSION

*"What surprised him most was the terrible, impossible gulf that lay between him and everyone else. They seemed to him to be a different species, and he looked at them and they at him with distrust and hostility."*

In *Crime and Punishment*, Fyodor Dostoevsky's Rashkolnikov, pushed beyond his limits and alienated from the collective body of humankind by his own feelings of insecurity, self-loathing, and weakness, plans and commits a murder in order to prove to himself that he is not a "nobody."

*Crime and Punishment* was published in 1866, which shows that feelings of alienation and hostility toward our fellow men are not just a recent phenomenon. Unfortunately, however, in today's society where individuals have become compartmentalized,

## CONCLUSION

catalogued, and numbered, the Rashkolnikov-type characters seem to increasingly be slipping between the cracks, especially with overworked and under financed mental health services. These people remain ignored and untreated until their frustrations force them to lash out and plaster themselves across our shared awareness in seemingly random acts of irrational violence.

Every time we hear of another killing rampage, whether it be a school shooting or movie theater rampage, we are left with the question of why. What prompts these spree killings, how can we prevent them, and how can we protect ourselves and our loved ones from the line of fire?

In most cases, a triggering event occurs which may be minor in nature for most people (such as breaking up with someone, getting laid off, being bullied at school) but for that individual it is the last straw; he/she reaches his/her breaking point and seeks revenge on those he/she perceives as responsible for his/her circumstances and bad luck.

Sometimes there is a history of mental health problems and in many cases, it appears the spree killer was starting to experience delusional thinking but it may not have been significant enough to warrant medical attention or intervention. Unfortunately, in many cases, those signs were seen and acknowledged but not acted upon due to an overcrowded mental health system as well as laws that prohibit anyone over the age of 18 to seek counseling or be placed in an in-house stay at a mental facility without their approval and agreement. In many cases, I suspect the rampage killer may have had some symptoms of schizophrenia.

Most mental-health experts say it's hard, if not impossible, to tell when someone is ill enough to go on a killing rampage and then shoot themselves.

Frequently, people will simply not talk. Alternatively, they will talk to someone who isn't really there, but in their heads. In addition, they are in a place so dark that sometimes the only escape they see is the killing of who is "causing" their unhappiness or suicide.

What can be seen as a common thread running through nearly all of these cases is that minor warnings signs were there as yellow flags, sometimes (in retrospect) red flags; however, they only became red flags when the blood was spilled.

Then there is the case of someone like Sabine Radmacher, a seemingly normal, intelligent woman who just snapped. In cases like these, it is important to remember some statistics. In any given year, roughly 22% of American adults suffer from a diagnosable mental disorder. Of them, about 5% have some form of depression and 1.5% have either bi-polar disorder or a form of schizophrenia. In today's economic climate, all stress-related versions of mental illness are on the rise. In the United States suicide is the 11$^{th}$ leading cause of death.

# CONCLUSION

## "TRIGGER" EVENTS THAT CAN CAUSE MAJOR STRESS

Being fired, laid off, suspended, or passed over for promotion

Disciplinary action, poor performance review, criticism from boss or coworkers

Bank or court action (foreclosure, restraining order, custody hearing)

Failed or spurned romance, personal crisis (divorce, death in family)

IMPORTANT! If you observe someone exhibiting behavior that you believe is threatening to himself or others, SPEAK TO A PROFESSIONAL ABOUT YOUR CONCERNS IMMEDIATELY.

Sadly, it seems that there is no easy solution to the increasing incidents of spree/rampage killers. The obvious solutions are more gun control and increased financial support for mental health services as well as more understanding and sympathy amongst the general public for those who are blighted by mental health issues, in an increasingly stressful world.

People don't "like" to talk about depression; they don't think of it as a real disease and, thus, either sweep it under the rug and ignore it .

Other people will go out of their way to avoid people with mental illness. Which can only add to the sufferers feelings of rejection and alienation by society.

It's time, we as a modern society, stop focusing on the aftermath of the mentally ill who are ignored and overlooked and start focusing on ways we can help them before they hurt themselves or someone else.

# TEENAGE GIRL KILLERS

What are little girls made of, made of?

What are little girls made of?

Sugar and spice, and everything nice,

That's what little girls are made of.

Murder is horrific whenever it happens and in what ever circumstances. But when a murder is carried out by a young girl, not much more than a child, it is doubly horrific. And it is seized upon by the popular press with a ghoulish fascination.

The teenage years are difficult for many girls, with erratic and volatile emotions, changing looks and body appearance, the transition from a girl to a woman. However, the majority of teenage girls cope, without resorting to killing.

## TEENAGE GIRL KILLERS

What is it that goes wrong in the lives and minds of these girls that grow up to be teenage killers? Girls who ruthlessly murder strangers, young children, parents, and others?"

In this short book, I have chosen six murder cases committed by teenage girls, each case vastly different from the others. And all tragically sad. As I included Brenda Spencer in Rampage Killers I have omitted her in this part of the compilation even though she was just a teenager.

# JULIET HULME AND PAULINE PARKER

Murder she writes. Murder she did. New York Times Bestseller British murder novelist, Anne Perry, who has sold more than 26 million books worldwide, was convicted of murder in a sensational New Zealand murder trial when she was just fifteen-years-old.

Anne Perry's books wrestle with questions of sin and repentance, as well as the price of forgiveness and redemption. As a writer, Anne Perry has been prolific having written more than 70 books. Her first, The Cater Street Hangman, was published in 1979.

In 1954, Anne Perry - then a 15-year-old called Juliet Hulme living in New Zealand - helped to bludgeon to death the mother of her friend, Pauline Parker. Both were convicted and sent to prison.

Anne Perry's identity became known in the resurgence of interest in the killing surrounding the release of Peter Jackson's 1994 film Heavenly Creatures, which was based on the 1954 case. Juliet Hulme aka Anne Perry was played by Kate Winslet. The film title was taken from an entry in Pauline Parker's diary where she wrote that she and Juliet were heavenly creatures who needn't heed the rules of mere mortals.

## JULIET HULME

Juliet Marion Hulme was born in Blackheath, London on October 28, 1938, the year before the start of WWII. She was the firstborn child of Dr. Henry Hulme and his glamorous and clever wife Hilda Hulme. Her father was a physicist and worked as the Chief Assistant at the Royal Observatory in Greenwich.

When Juliet was two-years-old, she suffered severe psychological trauma due to the London Blitz. For months after this, she suffered from horrendous nightmares. When Juliet was five in March of 1944 her brother Jonathon was born. Following this birth, her mother Hilda suffered from serious post-partum complications and had to be hospitalized. At the age of six, during the winter of 1944, Juliet contracted bronchitis which then became severe pneumonia, of which she nearly died. Over the next two years, she remained sickly and virtually housebound.

As a small child, Juliet was demanding, excitable, precocious, self-willed, and displayed an intolerance of criticism. She was also full of fantasy and found it hard to stop play-acting games even when her friends had become bored. Juliet liked to remain a fairy, or whatever fantasy figure, long after the game had finished.

## JULIET HULME AND PAULINE PARKER

Shortly after the end of the war, her father became the Scientific Advisor to the Air Ministry. In late 1946, when Juliet was eight, she once again contracted pneumonia. On her recovery, the family doctor advised that she be sent to a warmer climate. Her parents sent her to stay with a family in the Bahamas for 13 months.

Towards the end of 1947, her father was offered and accepted the job of Rector of Canterbury College in Christchurch, New Zealand. The family moved to New Zealand in October of 1948. In New Zealand, at the beginning of 1949, Juliet was sent away to a private boarding school in Hawke's Bay on the North Island. Juliet was very unhappy there and stayed less than a year. It must have seemed to the young Juliet that her parents were forever sending her away.

In Christchurch, considered the most English city outside of England, the family lived in a grand colonial house, known as the Ilam, the official residence of the Rector. The house sat near a meandering confluence of the river Avon on the western outskirts of Christchurch. It had spectacular gardens full of flowering shrubs and close by were horse paddocks and open grazing farmland.

Juliet attended the Ilam School, an elementary and junior school within walking distance of her home. When she finished junior school, she was sent to a private Anglican girls' school, St Margaret's. However, her parents, who had Juliet's IQ tested, which measured 170, did not feel that she was being stimulated academically at the school. The parents decided to send her to Christchurch Girls' High School, a much larger establishment where they felt she would be more likely stimulated intellectually.

Shortly after starting at Christchurch in 1952, Juliet made a best friend, Pauline Parker: a friendship that was to end in a horrifying tragedy that shocked the city of Christchurch and indeed the whole of New Zealand as well as much of the rest of the world.

*Juliet's home in Christchurch*

## PAULINE PARKER

Pauline Yvonne Parker was born on May 26, 1938 in Christchurch, New Zealand. She was the second daughter born to Herbert Detlev Rieper, 43, and Honorah Mary Parker, 29. Unusually for that day and age in conservative Christchurch, they never married. Three other children had been born to them: the first, a boy in 1936, died at birth, followed by Wendy Patricia Parker, born in March 1937, and the fourth child, Rosemary Parker, born in March 1949 was born with Down syndrome and placed in an institution, Templeton Farm, outside Christchurch, which was the "norm" at that time. Rosemary was visited regularly by her family and occasionally brought home for visits.

Herbert, Pauline's father, was a quiet man who worked as a manager for a wholesale fish business in Christchurch city, and her mother ran the family's slightly shabby, shambolic house at 31 Gloucester Street and took in boarders. The house, although bought by both Herbert and Honorah, was only in Honorah's name, and the children all took her surname. The reasons are unknown.

When Pauline was five, she developed osteomyelitis, inflammation of the bone marrow. She spent months in the hospital and over the course of three years suffered painful treatments and operations. While her sister Wendy, who was three years her senior, and other little girls were out playing, Pauline spent her time in bed. Here, she lost herself in reading and writing and let her imagination soar. Her parents worried she was becoming introverted; she seemed to enjoy writing more than conversing or communicating with them.

Once back at school, Pauline still suffered from chronic leg pain and walked with a slight limp, and so she was excused from physical games and activities. Pauline was described by her schoolteachers as a mature, serious, bright girl and an imaginative, gifted writer.

Although the Riepers were not a particularly religious family, her older sister Wendy and Pauline attended the East Belt Methodist Church and would often go on church-organized outings and holidays. When Pauline was eleven, she began attending the Christchurch Girls' High School with Wendy. The family house backed onto the grounds of the school. Here, at the age of thirteen, she met Juliet Hulme, a classmate, and her life became irrevocably changed.

**BEST FRIENDS**

Soon after meeting, Juliet and Pauline bonded. They were both highly intelligent, with vivid imaginations, and both loved to write. They were also both, due to the ill health they had suffered over the years, excused from sports lessons at school. While their other classmates played tennis and hockey, Juliet and Pauline lost themselves in their imaginations and writing novels together. They became inseparable and developed, over a short period of time, an obsessive devotion to each other. Neither girl had ever experienced such a friendship before.

Juliet was tall for her age, slim, self-confident, and was considered attractive with a pink-and-white complexion, slanting blue-grey aquamarine eyes, shoulder-length light brown hair, and

## JULIET HULME AND PAULINE PARKER

spoke with "a refined English accent." Pauline was shorter than Juliet, slightly dumpy, with dark curly hair, brown eyes, and an almost permanent angry scowl on her olive-skinned face.

Pauline was enamored by Juliet's house and sophisticated family lifestyle, so different from her own. Pauline would spend days on end at Juliet's house, where Juliet taught her how to ride her pony, an activity Pauline particularly enjoyed and would often remark that lameness did not matter when you were in the saddle. Pauline soon developed a real interest in horses and badgered her parents to buy her one. They refused, which led to Pauline being moody and ignoring them and spending more time than ever at Juliet's house. The two girls lived about three miles apart from each other, and Pauline would eagerly cycle the forty-five minutes it took to get her there even if in pain.

PAULINE PARKER     JULIET HULME

While initially both girls' sets of parents were pleased at the friendship, as its intensity grew it began to cause them concern. The girls were crazy about each other. When they were not with each other, they became moody and easy to anger. They began to build and share a rich fantasy life and lost themselves in a world of fictional characters as they fired each other's imaginations. They renamed themselves Gina (Pauline) and Deborah (Juliet) and insisted their families call them by these names. When they weren't together, they were talking on the telephone until told to free the line by their parents. By the end of 1952, they had both become prolific writers. At Juliet's house they would creep out into the gardens and reenact their fictional characters under the moonlight. To the girls, their fantasy life was more intense and more satisfying to them than reality.

In the spring of 1953, as Juliet's parents were planning a three-month trip back to England and leaving Juliet in the care of Pauline's family, Juliet was found to have tuberculosis in one lung. Fourteen-year-old Juliet was forced to spend four months in quarantine and isolation at the Cashmere Sanatorium in Port Hills, Christchurch. During this time, Juliet's only entertainment was reading, writing, her imagination, and the numerous daily letters from Pauline. Although Pauline's parents were concerned about Juliette, they were also relieved and hoped this forced separation would stop the intensity of the girl's friendship, which they were beginning to feel was abnormal.

## JULIET HULME AND PAULINE PARKER

*Juliet's Garden*

With Juliet in isolation in hospital, and Pauline spending more time at home, Pauline took interest in one of her mother's boarders: a young university student, Nicholas. Before long, fourteen-year-old Pauline was secretly sharing his bed until her father discovered them and threw Nicolas out of the house. Pauline did not share this one secret with Juliet.

When Dr. Hulme and his wife returned from England, Juliet was allowed to go home and recuperate. To aid in Juliet's recovery, Pauline was invited to stay more frequently at Ilam. The girls' relationship became even more intense. The girls considered themselves geniuses and were convinced that the "novels" they had written were truly brilliant. They decided that they must make their way to the then publishing capital of the world, New York, where their books, they were convinced, would be in great demand. They would then go to Hollywood and have their books made into movies. They created a list of their favorite movie stars who they called their "Saints." At night, according to Pauline's diary, they would spend time "enacting how each Saint would make love in bed." Pauline wrote after one such session, "We have now learned the peace of the thing called Bliss, the joy of the thing called Sin." They began to save for their trip to New York, and began shoplifting from Woolworth's and pilfering from their parents.

In 1953, the Hume's house began to receive another frequent figure, Walter Andrew Bowman Perry, a Canadian from Winnipeg. He had arrived in Christchurch on July 2, 1953, on an assignment for a British Company based in London, Associated Industrial Consultants. Within a short amount of time on arriving in Christchurch, he became introduced to the Hume's. They became great friends: Walter in particular with Hilda Hulme and by Christmas of 1953, he was living in a flat attached to the Hulme's house. Hilda and Walter (Bill) had fallen in love, and the three adults had decided to be "grown up" about it rather than distress the children with the truth: separations and divorces. All Henry Hulme asked off his wife was that she be discreet in front of the children and friends. However, the social circles within Christchurch that the Hulme's and Walter mixed were not very large and within time the unusual living arrangements generated significant gossip.

## JULIET HULME AND PAULINE PARKER

Juliet asked Walter to buy her horse and whether to appease her who knows, he paid her fifty pounds. He had become aware at this time of the girl's plans to go to New York as had her parents. Juliet's parents and Pauline's parents had a meeting where they all voiced their concerns about the girls' increasingly intense relationship. The girls had begun to bathe together, and Pauline would frequently spend all night in Juliet's bed. They all agreed it was unhealthy.

Things pretty much rattled on the same for another couple of months, with both sets of parents becoming increasingly concerned about their daughter's friendship. Honorah Parker became so concerned, especially at the hostility that Pauline was now showing her, her common law husband, and her sister Wendy that she took Pauline to see the family doctor, Dr. Bennett. Honorah told the doctor all about the girl's friendship. The doctor then examined Pauline and talked to her. Dr. Bennett then told Honorah that he suspected the girls of having a homosexual relationship.

Honorah met with the Hulme's and told them the doctor's opinion. Homosexuality was thought to be a serious mental illness at the time, so both sets of parents agreed to try to prevent the relationship from contining. At about the same time, Henry Hulme was asked to resign from his post as Rector of Canterbury College. Whether this was because of his unusual living arrangements, it's not entirely sure.

# TEENAGE GIRL KILLERS

*Pauline & Juliet*

By January of 1954, between them, the girls had written almost six novels, poetry, and an opera. Events after this began to happen in a rapid succession. During the Easter festivities of 1954, Juliet found her mother in bed with Walter. Although not entirely surprised, she had her suspicions, she was profoundly upset. Then her father, a few days later, announced to Juliet that he and her mother were getting divorced. Juliet felt like her world was crumbling around her. Pauline was equally devastated as by this time she felt like the Hulme's were her family as well. To top it all, Dr. Hulme told the children that he was returning to England to work with Sir William Penned in the British atomic research team. He informed them that Jonathan would accompany him back to England and they would travel via South Africa where Juliet, because of her health, would stay with his sister. He said the climate there would be beneficial for her. He said he had booked their tickets for the 3rd of July.

Juliette and Pauline were devastated. They could see the future they had planned for themselves in New York and Hollywood falling apart. Juliet said there was only one thing they could do: Pauline must come with her to South Africa. They decided that the money they had saved so far for their fares to New York would now be spent on Pauline's fare to South Africa. Juliet spoke with her parents and told them Pauline must accompany her to South Africa. They agreed as long as Pauline's mother would allow her. Both the Hulme knew full well that Honorah Parker would never agree to the plan, as they had already discussed it with her. They were right. Honorah Parker refused adamantly to give her permission but said she would offer no objection to the girls spending time together before Juliet's departure.

Both girls were determined not to be parted and felt intense anger and hate towards Honorah Parker, the only block they saw preventing Pauline leaving for South Africa. Pauline felt, that without her mother around, she could easily persuade her father. They were unaware that Pauline's parents and the Hulme's were collaborating in their efforts to separate them. Upon, Honorah's refusal, the two girls hatched a plan. On June 19, Pauline wrote in her diary:

"We practically finished our books today, and our main like for the day was to "moider*" mother. This notion is not a new one, but this time it is a definite plan which we intend to carry out. We have worked it all out and are both thrilled with the idea. Naturally, we feel a trifle nervous but the anticipation is great."

(*The term "moider" is the Brooklyn pronunciation of the word "murder that the girls had acquired from reading crime fiction.) The two girls had decided that the best way to end Pauline's mother's objections was to kill her in such a way that it would look accidental. On June 20th, Pauline wrote in her diary:

"Deborah and I talked for some time. Afterwards, we discussed our plans for 'moidering' Mother and made them clear. But peculiarly enough, I have no qualms of conscience. Or is it peculiar? We are so made."

The girls had decided to pretend to their prospective parents that they had resigned themselves to the separation. Pauline suggested to her mother that before Juliet left that she, her mother, and Juliet go for an afternoon walk and tea on June 22nd to Victoria Park in the Port Hills above Christchurch. Honorah, relieved at last that Pauline had resigned herself to Juliet's departure, happily agreed. On June 21st, Pauline wrote in her diary:

"Deborah rang, and we decided to use a brick in a stocking

rather than a sandbag. Mother has fallen in with plans beautifully. Feel quite keyed up."

The top of the page in her diary for June 22nd was headed in printed letters:

**"THE DAY OF THE HAPPY EVENT."**

The entry for this day read:

"I felt very excited last night and sort of 'night-before-Christmas,' but I did not have pleasant dreams. I am about to rise."

On June the 22nd, 1954, Juliet arrived at Pauline's house for a home-cooked lunch with Honorah, Herbert, Pauline's father, Pauline, and her sister Wendy. After lunch, when Herbert and Wendy had returned to work, Juliet and Pauline helped Honorah wash the dishes and tidy up. The three of them then dressed in warm coats, made their way to the bus stop to catch the bus up to Cashmere Hills, and then walked to Victoria Park.

Victoria Park is situated on the ridges and valleys descending from the Sugarloaf Mountain and has panoramic views of Christchurch, the Canterbury Plains, Pegasus Bay, and the Southern Alps. The park, popular with residents and tourists to Christchurch, has a huge array of paths for walking among the trees, shrubberies, and flowers. On arrival at the park, they made their way to a tea kiosk, where they enjoyed a cup of tea, before setting off for their walk.

At 3 p.m., the girls led Honorah down an isolated path through a wooded area. About 420ft down the path, Juliet, near a small wooden bridge dropped a pink stone. Honorah bent down to pick it up and as she did so, Pauline whipped out of her coat pocket a half brick stuffed in a stocking and bashed her mother over the back of the head. Startled, Honorah tried to ward of the blows as Pauline mercilessly bashed away. Honorah continued trying to fight, so Juliet yanked the brick laden stocking from Pauline and inflicted more furious blows. Blood was splattering all over the place as the girls took turns to bash Honorah to almost beyond recognition. When they were finished, the girls looked at each other slightly shocked and then ran back to the nearby tea kiosk.

A startled Agnes and Kenneth Ritchie watched the two visibly upset girls covered in blood running towards them.

"It's Mummy!" cried Pauline to Agnes Ritchie. "She's terrible! I think she's dead. We tried to carry her. She was too heavy."

"Yes, it's her mother!" Juliet gasped in a hysterical voice. "She's covered with blood!"

"We were coming back along the track. Mummy tripped on a plank and hit her head when she landed," sobbed Pauline. "She kept falling, and her head kept banging and bumping as she fell."

"I'll always remember her head banging," Juliet dramatically added.

## JULIET HULME AND PAULINE PARKER

Kenneth Ritchie ran off in the direction from which the girls had come. He found the bloody, battered body of Honorah. It looked like no accident to him. Upset, he made his way back to the kiosk and phoned the police and ambulance.

The ambulance arrived and took Honorah's corpse away. The police took a brief statement from the distraught girls before having them driven home to Juliet's house.

Upon searching the scene of the "accident," it did not take the police long to discover the torn, blood-soaked stocking with the brick. The girls' story of accidental death didn't add up.

The pathologist at the hospital, Colin Pearson, reported that there were forty-five external injuries – fractures to the front of the skull and twenty-four wounds to the face and scalp. He said that all of the injuries were consistent with being battered by the brick. There was also bruising on the throat indicating that she had been forcibly held by the neck.

The police realized they were dealing with a brutal murder and their prime suspects were Pauline Parker and Juliet Hulme.

The police went to the Hulme's house and interviewed the girls separately. After repeated questioning, the girls made full confessions, and they were taken into custody. As a result, both of the girls' bedrooms were searched, and Pauline's diary and writings were taken as evidence by the police. Mysteriously, no diary or writings by Juliet were found. It was speculated that her parents, or

Juliet herself, may have destroyed such items before the police arrived to arrest her.

*Pauline Parker Mug Shot*

At their first court appearance, a magistrate committed Juliet Hulme (at the age of 15-years, 10-months) and Pauline Parker (at the age of 16) for trial for the murder of Honorah Mary Parker. Both girls were then subjected to a battery of physical and psychological examinations in the six weeks between the murder and the trial.

Two weeks following the murder, while his daughter was in jail awaiting trial, Dr. Hulme and his son Jonathan departed for England, Honorah Parker lay buried in a Christchurch cemetery, and Hilda Hulme and Herbert Rieper were left to face the ordeal of the gaping crowds in court and the international media attention. Walter

## JULIET HULME AND PAULINE PARKER

Perry lent his full support to Hilda. When Dr. Hulme left for England, Hilda Hulme along, with Walter Perry, were evicted from the official residence of the Rector, Ilam. They sold what possessions they had to pay for Juliet's defense and went to live in Port Levy, the Hulme' holiday home twelve miles south of Christchurch city center.

The trial began on Monday, August 23rd, at the Supreme Court of New Zealand before Justice Adams; a trial that aroused great interest not only in Christchurch but internationally as well.

Pauline and Juliet pled not guilty due to insanity.

The prosecution described the crime,

"As a coldly, callously-planned murder committed by two highly intelligent and sane but precocious and dirty-minded little girls."

They introduced extracts from Pauline's diaries to illustrate their argument. The lawyers for both girls based their defense upon insanity and introduced a number of psychiatrists to testify.

Dr. Medlicott, the psychiatrist for the defense, said that Juliet and Pauline had developed paranoia of an exalted type in a setting of folie a deux, a communicative form of insanity.

"They presented gross conceit and arrogance, were exalted in mood, held ideas of a grandiose delusional nature, and showed gross reversal of moral values."

Dr. Medlicott also testified that when he questioned Juliet as to whether she had had sexual relations with Pauline she had replied,

"But how could we? We are both women."

The trial lasted for nearly six days ending on August 28th, 1954. The jury took just two hours and twelve minutes to reject Juliet and Pauline's plea of insanity and found them guilty of murder.

### SENTENCING

Before sentencing, Justice Adams asked Juliet and Pauline if they had anything they wished to say. Neither girl responded. The girls, who showed no signs of emotion, were then sentenced.

Justice Adams addressed the girls,

"You both being held to be under the age of 18, the sentence of the court is detention at her Majesty's pleasure. That sentence is passed upon each of you."

As Juliet and Pauline were under the age of eighteen, they were excluded from being considered for the death penalty under the country's laws at that time. The sentence meant that they were to be detained (indefinitely) at the discretion of the Minister of Justice. The trial was Juliet's and Pauline's last time together; it was to be a permanent separation. The two girls were incarcerated in separate prisons.

The general public was outraged by the crime and, even more

so, by the seemingly unrepentant attitude of the two girls. The public wanted a harsher punishment meted out to them. Juliet and Pauline were purposefully separated, as it was perceived that it would be the most severe punishment for them. They were allowed no form of communication whatsoever. The Minister of Justice ordered regular reports on their progress during their incarceration. Juliet was regarded by the public to have been the dominant partner in the friendship and consequently received the harshest treatment.

Following the conclusion of the trial, Mrs. Hulme changed her name by deed poll to Mrs. Hilda Perry and left New Zealand on September 11th, 1954 with Walter Perry and returned to England. Once her divorce from Dr. Hulme was finalized, she and Walter married and settled permanently in England.

**IMPRISONMENT JULIET**

Juliet was imprisoned in Auckland's notorious Mt Eden Prison, which contained in separate wings both female and male inmates. It had the reputation of been the toughest prison in the southern hemisphere. She was the only child inmate. It was also the only prison in New Zealand where capital punishment was carried out. Mt Eden Prison construction had begun in the late 1800s, and its design was based on the belief, prevalent at that time, that prisons should be unpleasant, grim places to be dreaded.

Here, the fifteen-year-old spent her first three months in a tiny cell in solitary confinement. When released from solitary confinement, she was assigned to hard labor work but collapsed after two weeks. She was then sent to work sewing uniforms. The first few months of Juliet's imprisonment conditions were grim and harsh.

Many years later, Juliet said in an interview,

"The prison was raw and brutal -- no fruit and no library. It was cold, and there were rats, canvas sheets, and calico underwear. I had to wash out my sanitary towels by hand."

During the time she was there, four evening executions were held on the prison's steel scaffold in the central yard. As time wore on, conditions became easier for her by the intervention of The Howard League for Penal Reform. She was allowed to resume her studies and took and passed, with high grades, her high school exams in History, English, Geography, and Latin and passed her University Entrance exams.

Former academic colleagues of her father's were allowed to visit and tutor her. No family member visited her while she was incarcerated, and their correspondence with her was very infrequent. Former classmates and family friends did, however, visit. Juliet spent five and a half years in Mt. Eden before being transferred to the Arohata Borstal, (Juvenile Detention Center) outside Wellington.

Towards the end of 1959, shortly after her twenty-first birthday, Juliet was secretly released from prison, furnished with an anonymous new identity, and deported out of the country. She was put on a flight to Rome and met by her father who took her to England. Juliet Hulme's release was made public two weeks after her deportation.

## IMPRISONMENT PAULINE

Pauline was sent to the Arohata Borstal (Juvenile Detention Center) outside of Wellington, New Zealand's capital city. As can be imagined, Pauline's relationship with her family following the murder was virtually non-existent. Her father, Herbert Rieper, was not present at her conviction or sentencing. He had made bitter statements about Pauline to the press following the trial. He only made one visit to her during her incarceration, and that is believed to have been their last communication.

During her time in Arohata Borstal, she converted to Roman Catholicism and became a devout Catholic. Pauline also studied for her school certificate and passed her high school graduation exams in Drawing and Design, English, French, Mathematics, Latin, and, later, Maori. She then went on to pass her University Entrance exams and began a Bachelor of Arts degree, which she completed after leaving prison.

Before Juliet was moved to Arohata Borstal, Pauline was transferred to Paparua Prison, near Christchurch. Here, she was visited by family and friends.

After Juliet had been deported from New Zealand, Pauline was given a new identity and released on parole. During this time, she was closely monitored. She enrolled at Auckland University and completed her BA and then trained as a librarian. When her parole time was up in 1965, Pauline left New Zealand and moved to England.

**PAULINE IN ENGLAND**

In England, Pauline settled in Kent under her new name of Hilary Nathan. Here, she did a teachers' training course and took a job teaching mentally handicapped children at Abbey Court special school in Strood where she eventually became deputy headmistress.

When Pauline retired, she moved to the little village of Hoo near Rochester in Kent and opened a children's riding school. Pauline lived in a sparsely furnished little three-bedroom cottage with no radio or television but a living room full of dolls and a large rocking horse. Every weekend, six young girls from the village would muck out the stables behind the cottage where Pauline kept her ponies. She was also a regular worshipper at the English Martyrs' Roman Catholic Church in Rochester.

Pauline's, aka Hilary's, quiet life was shattered when the film Heavenly Creatures was released in 1994 and reporters tracked her down. When a reporter turned up on her doorstep, Pauline, brushing down the horses and dressed in gumboots and anorak, denied she was Pauline Parker and said,

"I have absolutely no comment to make."

# JULIET HULME AND PAULINE PARKER

*Pauline Parker in Kent*

Joyce Hookins, her next-door neighbor, said,

"She was a very quiet woman and always very business-like in her dealings with people. She always seemed very nice and clearly loved children. She never talked about her past, and no one had any idea she was even from New Zealand."

Members of the church where she worshipped were astounded to learn of Hilary Nathan's past.

"It's so difficult to believe," said one woman. "She seems like such a good woman. This is a terrible shock to us all."

Her sister Wendy told reporters that her sister was living the life she had always dreamed of as a girl: to own a place in the country and have a stable of horses and that Pauline deeply regretted what she had done and was now so repentant, she spent most of her time praying.

Over the years, Wendy and Pauline have written regularly, and Pauline sends money for her nephews in New Zealand. Wendy chose never to confront sister about what she had done. She believes Pauline didn't fully understand the finality of death.

"Well, it was absolutely overboard, wasn't it?" She said.

With her identity uncovered, Pauline, aka Hilary, moved to the cold, remote sparsely populated island of Burray in Orkney, Scotland in 1997, almost as far north as she could go to escape her past. Here she lives a solitary existence in a small cottage in Burray and teaches children to ride. She attends the Catholic Church in Kirkwall every Sunday. Her sister Wendy commented to a reporter,

"She committed the most terrible crime and has spent sixty years repaying it by keeping away from people and doing her own thing."

### JULIET IN ENGLAND

When Juliet returned to England, she went to live with her mother and stepfather Walter Perry, whose surname she had adopted as her new identity, Anne Perry.

From 1962 and 1964, she worked for a while as an air stewardess in Northumberland, England before taking a job from 1964 to 1966 as an assistant buyer for a department store in Newcastle, England. When she had saved enough money to fulfill her childhood dream of moving to America, Anne left for California. She arrived during the summer of love in 1967 at the age of twenty-nine and became a property underwriter for a company in Los Angeles.

While living in California, Anne was introduced by an acquaintance to the Church of Jesus Christ of Latter Day Saints and became a Mormon. Anne had never given up her dream of becoming a writer and while working during the day, she spent her evenings writing without obtaining any commercial success. She found Los Angeles with its glitzy, frantic lifestyle a difficult one in which to write. However, Anne remained in Los Angeles working a variety of jobs. When she learned that her stepfather was seriously ill, she returned to England in 1972 to help her mother. For a while, she lived with her mother and Walter in Watford. Then her father, Henry Hulme, gave her a small amount of money to buy a house and a small living allowance to allow her to concentrate on her writing.

She found a small run-down thatched-roof terraced cottage, known as the fox cottages, in the small village of Darsham, Suffolk, just north of the Darsham Marshes, a nature reserve and a few miles inland from the cold North Sea coast. Here, she camped as she renovated the cottage doing the major part of the renovation work herself. With the renovations complete, she was now absolutely determined to devote herself to writing. She wrote relentlessly except for when she attended the Church of Jesus Christ of Latter Day Saints in the nearby town of Lowestoft, which had opened in the 1840's.

With each manuscript finished, she would send it off to publishers and wait eagerly for the response. With each rejection letter, she would sink into a depression and would then begin on her next book. Her books at this stage were mainly historical novels. She then wrote her first murder mystery, "The Cater Street Hangman," which was accepted for publication and published in 1979.

At last, Anne Perry/Juliet Hulme had reached her lifetime ambition at the age of thirty-nine of becoming a published author. With her first success, she proceeded to work at a furious pace to build up her readership and her reputation. With her literary success, particularly in America, came financial rewards. Anne moved to Portmahomack, a tiny coastal village on the eastern coast of Scotland, fifty miles north of Inverness, where her mother had moved following Walter Perry's death. She bought a barn overlooking the sea and renovated it into a luxurious home. The village, a small, close-knit community, has only about five hundred permanent residents.

When the film "Heavenly Creatures" was released in 1994, an astute New Zealand journalist revealed to the world that the famous murder mystery novelist, Anne Perry, was the teenage murderer Juliet Hulme. When the news first broke, Anne was publishing her 19th book. Anne was petrified that it would destroy her career as a writer. She said in an interview,

"It seemed so unfair; everything I had worked to achieve as a decent member of society was threatened and once again my life was being interpreted by someone else. It had happened in court when, as a minor, I wasn't allowed to speak, and I heard all these lies being told and now there is a film, but nobody had bothered to interview me before filming. I knew nothing about the movie until the day before its release. All I could think of was that my life would fall apart and that it might kill my mother."

However, the revelation that Anne wrote from personal experience as a murderer proved lucrative for sales. Disproving, in Anne Perry's case, the old age adage that crime doesn't pay.

Since then she has given numerous interviews over the years to promote her books and has never displayed much remorse. Anne Perry believes she has paid her debt to society.

In 2006, Amanda Cable of the English Daily Mail newspaper asked Anne if she ever thought back to the murder. She replied,

"No ... I would just torment myself and that wouldn't help anyone."

She was asked did she ever think of her victim?

"No," Anne said. "She was somebody I barely knew."

In the film "Heavenly Creatures," Pauline and Juliet were portrayed as lesbians. Anne, in an interview, stated in March of 2006 that while her relationship with Pauline was obsessive, they were not lesbians.

## EXCERPTS FROM ANNE PERRY'S BOOKS

### The Hyde Park Headsman

"Well, it's not very difficult to hit someone on the head, if they trust you and are not expecting anything of the sort."

### Resurrection Row

"Actually to kill someone, you have to care desperately over something, whether it is hate, fear, greed or because they stand in the way between you and something you hunger for."

### Rutland Place

# JULIET HULME AND PAULINE PARKER

"[Murder is] a double tragedy - not only for the victim and those who cared for her, but for the murderer also, and whoever loved or needed or pitied the tormented soul...[For] society was cruel; it seldom forgave, and it never, ever forgot."

In "**A Sudden and Fearful Death**," Perry has a character say:

"We all try to forget what hurts us; it is sometimes the only way we can continue."

What I find quite extraordinary is that both women, who committed a brutal horrifying murder on the other side of the world, have both chosen to settle in Scotland, approximately one hundred miles from each other, where they both spend, on the whole, very reclusive lives.

Anne Perry, when learning that Pauline Parker lived so close, said she had no plans to contact her. Pauline, who has no radio or television or any other modern types of communication, might not even be aware that her best friend who helped murder her mother for her, lives in Scotland.

# CHERYL PIERSON

The family living at 293 Magnolia Drive in the quiet suburb of Seldon on Long Island's North Shore seemed almost like the perfect all American family. James and Cathleen Pierson, a petite brunette, lived here with their son Jim, born in 1966, and two daughters Cheryl, born in 1969, and Jo Ann, born in 1977. James and Cathleen had married in 1965, barely three years out of high school.

James was a hard working electrician and supervisor for an electronics company in the nearby town of Huntington as well as being a partner in a lucrative cable television company.

To the community, James Pierson seemed to be a good family man, if not perhaps a bit of a loudmouth and slightly obnoxious. He coached the local Little League where his son played, and he and Cathleen went bowling on Thursday nights. He was regarded as being financially generous to his wife and three children. He bought his wife a brand new Lincoln Continental with the license plate CATHLEEN in which Cathleen proudly drove her children around. He was also a strict disciplinarian to his children and taught them from an early age to be quiet when adults entered a room, to help with household chores, and always to say "please" and "thank you." When they obeyed him, he would be generous with gifts. When they disobeyed him, his children knew him as having a violent temper.

The comfortable pleasant family life became shattered when Cathleen became seriously ill with a grave kidney disease in 1979. At this time, Jim Jr. had just turned thirteen, Cheryl was ten, and JoAnn just two years old.

Cathleen, for nearly six years, required regular dialysis and hospitalization and underwent two kidney transplants before dying, at the age of thirty-eight in 1985.

During the six years of James Pierson's wife's illness, despite the help from his mother Virginia Pierson and sister Marilyn Adams, the young Cheryl, as the eldest daughter, took on many of the household responsibilities such as caring for her younger sister, JoAnn, and dying mother. She began to feel important in the household, as for the first time in her life, her busy father began to seem to notice and appreciate her. Cheryl reveled in her father's attention.

Despite the problems at home with her mother's declining health, Cheryl was a popular, happy, go-lucky girl at Newfield High School, the kind of girl everyone wanted to know. She was an attractive brunette with an easy sense of humor. As she progressed into her teen years, she became a cheerleader. She was a girl all the boys wanted to go out with, while the girls envied her clothing, appearance, and seemingly effortless charm. Cheryl seemed destined to have everything she wanted. One word frequently used by acquaintances to describe Cheryl was, "Sweet."

Meanwhile, James Pierson's relationship with his son Jim, as he moved into his teen years, deteriorated.

Jim grew his hair long and wore earrings, which caused his father to call him a fag, although he was totally heterosexual. Jim also had aspirations to become a musician and became a keen drum player, driving his father mad with "his racket." All these activities were completely alien to James who believed in children learning a trade. James would frequently lash out at Jim with his fists.

Jim, unable to withstand his father's aggression towards him, moved out of the family home in 1984, shortly after his eighteenth birthday, and took a low paying job at the Stony Brook Hospital. He still visited the family home to visit his mother and sisters and would occasionally join them all for a family dinner.

Around about the time Jim moved out, Cheryl, now fifteen, began dating Rob Cuccio. He was her first serious boyfriend, was two years her senior, and another Long Island teenager. As James was such a strict disciplinarian, he would not allow Cheryl to go out on dates with Rob but insisted instead that they stay at home where he could keep an eye on them and never left the two of them on their own. The two young teenagers found the situation frustrating but complied. They spent hours on the telephone and left presents for each other in their lockers at school.

When Cheryl's mother died on February 13th, 1985, James relented slightly and allowed Cheryl out on a Saturday night provided she was home by eleven. For her sixteenth birthday, James hosted a lavish sweet-16 birthday party for Cheryl. All her friends, family, and close neighbors attended the event. The family presented a warm, close-knit unit, despite the sad loss of Cathleen just three months before. James and Jim appeared to be getting on slightly better, both father and son making an effort.

Just nine months later on the snowy, chilly, dark, early morning of February 5th 1986, James, at the age of forty-two, closed his front door and headed for his truck to drive to work. Just as he was about to unlock the vehicle door, a rifle bullet slammed into his back, the force of which caused him to fall against the truck before falling to the ground. As James lay on the driveway, a young man approached his bleeding form and shot James four more times in the head.

Inside the house, Cheryl's alarm went off, and she clambered out of bed. The family's toy poodle excitedly barked wanting to be let out. Cheryl went downstairs dressed in her pajamas to open the front door to let out the dog. As she opened the front door, the first thing that caught her attention was the body of her father lying in the driveway. She hurried back upstairs and put on a track suit before rushing outside and running next door to her neighbors' house, Michael and Alberta Kosser, for help.

Michael called the Suffolk County Police Department and told them that his neighbor was hurt. Michael had thought he had slipped and fallen on the ice.

Then Michael hurried outside and attempted to staunch the flow of blood from James's head and chest. The police and ambulance soon appeared on the scene. The ambulance men turned Pierson's body over hoping to apply mouth-to-mouth resuscitation, but it was too late: James was dead. It did not take them too long to realize that it was no accident but a cold blooded murder.

Detectives from the homicide division arrived, and the area was cordoned off with yellow crime scene tape. Detectives began searching for clues and for who would want to murder James Pierson. It looked to them like a professional hit.

They first began investigating his finances. They discovered his estate was worth about $500,000 and would be inherited by Jim, Cheryl, and eight-year-old JoAnn.

They next began investigating his work background and interviewing his work colleagues. There appeared to be no obvious enemies there.

James's funeral took place on a cold, snowy day, a few days after his murder, and nearly a year to the day of Cathleen's death, at the Holy Sepulchre cemetery in Coram. The three children sat quietly in a front pew as the priest delivered his ceremony. Eight-year-old JoAnn, who had lost both her parents in the space of a year, sat between her older brother and sister with tears streaming down her cheeks. On the other side of Cheryl sat her boyfriend Rob Cuccio. Cheryl held onto his hand as she cried quietly. About two hundred and fifty people attended the funeral, along with detectives observing the congregation. At the closing of the service, the priest read out a eulogy penned by Cheryl and Jim entitled "Our Dad."

In this, they recalled her father's strong will and also his soft heartedness. They wrote, "He was our best friend, as well as our dad…….." By which time most of the mourners were in tears.

Witnesses later said that Cheryl kissed her father's coffin and was inconsolable at his grave.

The detectives, upon questioning family, friends, and neighbors of the family, learned of the rift between Jim and his father. He immediately became a suspect, although he had an iron-clad alibi as he was at work when the murder took place. He was, however, taken in for questioning.

During the interview, when asked if he knew who had killed his father, he said he had no idea. However, he mentioned to the detectives that his younger sister Cheryl had mentioned wanting to kill her father during the Christmas festivities at the family home in 1985 and had even asked him if he knew a hit-man. He had dismissed it as foolish talk and anger at their father's strictness for not allowing her to spend more time with her boyfriend Rob and the occasional beatings she endured. He told her to hang in there; she would be old enough to leave home soon. He'd survived the abuse and she would, too. He said Cheryl had expressed concern for JoAnn and was worried her father would begin to beat her, too. The perfect family was beginning to disintegrate before the detectives' eyes.

A day later, the detectives got another lead.

They received an anonymous phone call that Cheryl had been asking around Newfield High School about how to hire a hit-man and that a fellow classmate of Cheryl's, Sean Pica, had said he would murder someone for $1000.

The detectives decided to pick up Sean Pica, who was sixteen and the son of Benjamin Pica, a former New York City police officer, for questioning. Sean was Cheryl's classmate, friend, and a Boy Scout with dental braces. At the time the police picked him up, he had a steady girlfriend and was planning to represent his high school in a carpentry competition. His parents were divorced and at the time of his arrest, he lived with his mother Joanne DelVecchio, who was a nurse, and a younger brother.

Sean, under questioning, quickly confessed to having shot James Pierson. He said that Cheryl had confided in him that her father had been sexually abusing her since she was eleven years old, shortly after her mother became ill, and that she was terrified he would begin doing the same thing to her younger sister JoAnn. Sean said that at first he didn't think she was serious about having him killed but after repeated conversations he realized she was. She agreed to pay him a $1000. He said the first $400 was paid to him the day after he did the shooting by Cheryl's boyfriend Rob Cuccio. Sean said it was not about the money but about helping a friend who saw no way out other than by exterminating her father to save her younger sister.

Later that night, detectives arrested Cheryl Pierson and Rob Cuccio. Like Sean, Rob was also the son of a former New York City policeman. Under questioning, the two teenagers rapidly confessed to their part in the conspiracy to kill James Pierson.

Rob said he had no part in hiring Sean; he had simply handed over the money to Sean at Cheryl's request. She had removed the money from her father's safe. He confessed that Cheryl had confided in him that her father was sexually abusing her and that she was terrified he would do the same to her little sister JoAnn. He said he had tried to talk about Cheryl's abuse to his father, but no one wanted to know.

Cheryl told the police that her father had been sexually abusing her since she was eleven, shortly after her mother became ill. She claimed the abuse started with wrestling and touching and that when she was fourteen he had sexual intercourse with her whilst her ill mother slept on the sofa in the living room. She said that the more time she spent out of the home with her boyfriend she had become increasingly concerned about her sister, as frequently she would return home and find her father wrestling with JoAnn on the sofa, and it reminded her of how the abuse had started with her.

When the detectives asked her why she had told no one in authority, she said that she was embarrassed and did not think anyone would believe her. She was also terrified that her father would be contacted.

While Cheryl was in custody, a medical examination revealed that she was pregnant. She claimed to detectives that it was her father's child.

At the first court appearance of the three teenagers for conspiracy to commit murder, they all plead not guilty, and all three were granted bail of varying amounts.

The teenagers quickly made media headlines around the country.

Rob Cuccio returned to live with his parents. Sean went to live with his father Benjamen and stepmother Karenanne in the suburb of Valley Stream.

The community of Seldon was deeply shocked when Cheryl, Sean Pica, and Rob Cuccio were arrested and even more so when the motive for the murder was revealed. Cheryl's allegations about her father polarized the community of Selden and her family.

Neither her paternal grandmother, Virginia Pierson, nor her aunt, Marilyn Adams, believed her story. Her brother Jim, having been physically abused by his father, believed her 100%. He said,

"Of course I believe her. How could she make something like that up?"

Cheryl was released into the custody of her aunt Marilyn Adams, her father's sister, who had been appointed guardian of both Cheryl and Joann. Given the accusations that Cheryl was making against her father, relations between Cheryl and Marilyn were, to put it minimally, strained. Marilyn thought Cheryl was a manipulative liar who had made up the story for reasons ranging from rebellion against her father's violent discipline to wanting his money.

Cheryl managed to get her living arrangements changed to live with her neighbors, Michael and Alberta Kosser, who had been close friends of her mother's. While staying with the Kosser's, Cheryl suffered a miscarriage. On examination of the fetus, it was found that the DNA matched that of Rob Cuccio and not that of James Pierson. To those who believed that Cheryl was lying about the abuse, this was the final proof that they were right.

By this time, a Suffolk County Grand Jury had returned second-degree murder indictments against Cheryl and Sean. Under New York state criminal laws, sixteen-year-olds charged with murder were automatically treated as adults and if found guilty faced minimum prison sentences of fifteen years.

Rob Cuccio, in a plea agreement, was given a lesser charge of solicitation for his part in the murder in return for his agreeing to be a prosecution witness. He was assured he would receive only a sentence of probation.

Rob apparently told Cheryl of his decision,

"What good would I be to you in jail?"


The judge in charge of the case had the discretion in the case of sixteen year olds of treating them as youthful offenders when the sentencing would be considerably lighter or as adults. As Sean and Cheryl attempted to lead normal lives, as much as possible in the circumstances, their attorneys and the prosecuting attorney attempted to make certain deals.

On March the 24th, 1987, Cheryl and Sean appeared in the Riverhead court in front of Judge Sherman and pleaded guilty to manslaughter and gave up their rights of trial by jury. There would be no trial. Cheryl was allowed to go home on continued bail pending sentencing while the judge ordered a Probation Department Report.

# CHERYL PIERSON

*Cheryl Pierson*

Sean had his bail revoked and was taken to the Suffolk Correctional Center. On April the 28th, he appeared in front of Judge Sherman again for sentencing. Judge Sherman had decided he should be tried as an adult. The prosecutor in the case alleged that Sean was a drugged-up sociopath with a $200-a-day cocaine habit. A psychiatrist told the court that he was an irrational little Rambo bent on saving a girl in trouble.

Judge Sherman called him a hired killer and sentenced him to eight to twenty-four years in prison. For the next sixteen years, Sean became known as 87-B-811 in the New York State prison system.

The media described him as the "Homeroom Hit Man."

While Judge Sherman was waiting for the probation report on Cheryl, he received hundreds of letters from around the country

## TEENAGE GIRL KILLERS

pleading for leniency towards Cheryl. These were mainly letters from sexual abuse victims.

While waiting for sentencing, Cheryl gave an interview to journalists describing her relationship with her father and the events leading to the murder. Cheryl claimed that her father would invite her to his bedroom to watch television together. Here, he would invite her into his bed and cuddle up under the covers. At first, she thought he was just been affectionate but at some stage, she couldn't remember when, she realized her father's advances were wrong. She didn't know how to handle the situation, her mother was dying, and although she hated what her father was doing to her, she still loved him. She said he began having sexual intercourse with her when she was fourteen. When she began to object and threatened her father that she would tell someone, he told her no one would believe her and she would regret it. She claimed that she didn't tell anyone in authority because she thought no one would believe her.

It is estimated that in the United States today, twenty-four percent of all children are abused at some time between birth through the age of twenty-two via some form of emotional abuse, physical abuse, sexual abuse, abandonment, or neglect. When the abuse occurs, it's more likely to be by someone who the child knows, including relatives or friends of the family, than by a stranger.

Children who have been, or are being, abused will frequently be very confused and unsure about what to do and who to tell.

## CHERYL PIERSON

The abuser will normally go to great lengths to keep their behavior a secret. They may use threats to the child if the child tells. They often also play on guilt and may persuade the child that it was all his/her fault and that he/she really wanted it to happen.

Only a small percentage of children who are being abused find the courage to tell someone.

The Suffolk County Probation report Judge Sherman ordered on Cheryl advised that she should be sentenced as a youthful offender. He set a date for a pre-sentencing hearing.

At the hearing, fourteen people testified that they had suspected something not quite right was going on between father and daughter. Michael Kosser, explaining his inaction to the judge said,

"I thought I had the evil mind." He continued by saying James was, "Always pinching, pulling her hair, fondling her, and rubbing her bottom."

One classmate of Cheryl's, Diana Ebentraut, testified that she had told her guidance counselor at school of her suspicions, but the counselor had done nothing. The counselor had told her that she couldn't take her word for it and that,

"Cheryl will have to tell me about it."

Jim Pierson testified about his childhood, which he described as been filled with emotional and physical abuse from his father. He said no matter what he did, he could never satisfy his father. When the prosecuting attorney asked him what he would have done if he had known his father was sexually abusing Cheryl he replied,

"I probably would have killed my father myself."

Cheryl also testified, telling the court that her father had begun to sexually abuse her when she was eleven years old and from the age of fourteen had been having sexual intercourse with her, frequently forcing her to have sex with him twice a day.

Cheryl said that she had become her father's surrogate wife. She said she was afraid to tell anybody what was happening.

"He brought me in his room. I put a pillow over my face to block it out until it was over. He always threatened me and said that nobody would believe me because I had no proof."

Cheryl said she loved her father and could not understand how he could be at once so generous to her and yet so cruel.

At the end of the hearing, the prosecutor Edward C. Jablonski argued for a substantial prison sentence as even if Cheryl was sexually abused by her father, of which there was no proof, the real issue was that she should be punished for taking her father's life rather than going to the police as, "that's what they're there for."

Cheryl's lawyer, Paul Gianelli, argued for leniency and a non-custodial sentence, arguing that Cheryl had suffered enough as a victim of incest and rape and that her act of having her father killed was an act of self-defense.

# CHERYL PIERSON

The judge, Justice Harvey Sherman, who believed that Cheryl had been sexually abused by her father, sentenced Cheryl to six months in jail and five years of probation. Cheryl, upon hearing the sentence, fainted. It took several minutes to revive her and once revived she was led from the courtroom sobbing and taken directly to jail.

That night Newsweek photographed Rob Cuccio tying a yellow ribbon around an old oak tree in his front yard with the promise that he would tie one there every day until Cheryl was free.

Cheryl spent fifteen weeks in prison. The day she was released, she was picked up outside the Suffolk County Correctional Facility by her brother Jim and Rob Cuccio in a white stretch limousine. The two young men took Cheryl for a celebratory breakfast and a drive around town. That afternoon Rob Cuccio proposed to Cheryl, a proposal Cheryl accepted. In the evening, they had a celebration dinner at the Cuccio family home.

Nine months later in October of 1988, Cheryl and Rob married.

Today, Rob and Cheryl remain married and have two daughters. They remain living on Long Island in Medford.

Sean Pica spent sixteen years in various state prisons. He was paroled from Sing Sing Correctional Facility in December of 2002. In an interview after his release he said,

"I was a very confused, mixed-up kid. I really didn't think of the repercussions. I thought I was helping a friend."

While in prison, Sean received his high school diploma, a Bachelor's Degree, and a Master's Degree. On leaving prison, he studied for a degree in social work. He then secured himself a job as a counselor with a nonprofit agency that helps ex-convicts adjust to life on the outside, troubled kids, and others in need of help.

## PARENTAL ABUSE

Reported instances of the abuse of children by their parents continue to rise and, for many in our society incest remain the unspeakable, often inarticulate taboo.

Children and teens who have been abused feel many different and overwhelming emotions, including:

### Fear

- Of the abuser
- Of losing adults important to them
- Of being taken away from home
- Of causing trouble

### Anger

- At the abuser
- At other adults around them who didn't protect them

- At themselves (feeling as if they caused trouble)
- Because they feel alone in the experience
- Because they have trouble talking about the abuse

**Sadness**

- About having something taken from them
- About being betrayed by someone they trusted

**Guilt**

For not being able to stop the abuse

About being involved in the experience

About their bodies response to the abuse (for example, if they found fondling pleasurable)

For believing they "consented" to the abuse (no child is capable of consent)

For "telling" - if they told

For keeping the secret - if they did not tell

**Confusion**

- Because their feelings change all the time
- Because they may still love and care about the abuser

# HOLLY HARVEY AND SANDRA KETCHUM

Carl and Sarah Collier married in 1951 and lived in the residential community of Riverdale, thirteen miles south from metropolitan Atlanta, in a white-brick ranch-style house on Plantation drive, a countrified tree-lined street. Carl worked as a Delta Air Lines maintenance worker and Sarah was a housewife. The couple were devout Christians and were important members of the congregation of the First Baptist Church.

Carl and Sarah had not been able to have children of their own and so in 1965 had adopted a boy, Kevin, and in 1967 a slightly younger girl by a year, Carla. Kevin Collier had been a source of joy to the Colliers. He had been a class A student, graduated from college, and followed his father's footsteps by working for Delta Airlines. Carla, on the other hand, became a rebellious hotheaded teenager who was a high-school dropout and, over the years, was jailed on three occasions for alcohol and drug violations. According to her brother, Kevin, she was continually arguing with her parents over her choice of friends and her drug and alcohol use. She ran away from home at the age of seventeen and took up with a petty crook, Gene Harvey.

## HOLLY HARVEY AND SANDRA KETCHUM

In March of 1989, Carla gave birth to a baby girl she named Holly. Gene and Carla separated when Holly was eighteen-months-old and Gene played little part in Holly's life after that. Carla, with the small toddler, returned to her parents' home for a short while. However, inevitably, Carla and her mother began to quarrel again, and Carla and Holly soon moved out.

As a child, Holly was well-behaved and considered very sweet. Her grandparents, Carl and Sarah, and her Uncle Kevin adored her. Her godmother, Anita Beckom, described her as a "beautiful, bright, playful, smart, happy little girl."

Carla found work as a dancer at a topless bar, the Crazy Horse Saloon, close to Atlanta's Hartsfield-Jackson airport. While she was out working, her then boyfriend, Scott Moore, would babysit Holly. When Holly was thirteen, her mother was busted for marijuana and sentenced to time in jail; she was out, however, within a few months, but it felt devastating to Holly. Carla's old school friend and Holly's godmother, Anita Beckom, took Holly in.

Holly, at this stage, was a student at Fayetteville Middle School. Here, she met Sandra Ketchum, who was a year older than she. The two girls instantly connected. They both came from dysfunctional homes. Sandra's mother had abandoned her as a baby and since then she had had three stepmothers. The first one died from a fatal illness, and the second one had abused her. When she met Holly, she was living with her father, Tim Ketchum, and her latest stepmother, Elizabeth, in an apartment complex in downtown Fayetteville.

Not only did the girls bond emotionally and mentally, they also felt a tremendous physical attraction towards each other. Holly began spending a large amount of time at Sandra's house. Tim Ketchum, Sandra's father, later recalled that Holly was possibly the nicest kid he'd ever met. In April of 2002, the two girls became lovers. They spent every moment they could together. When they were apart, they would write long, passionate letters to each other. Within a short time, their affair became known about at school, and the girl's were branded and taunted publicly as 'Dykes!' 'Lesbians!' and 'Queers!' This was a situation both girls found unbearable. They started to play hooky from school and would hang out in the nearby woods and smoke marijuana. Marijuana offered the girls a respite from school and family and they soon began experimenting with other drugs like methamphetamine when they could get it and cocaine when they could afford it.

Carla Harvey was arrested again in April of 2004 for marijuana possession with intent to sell. She was sentenced to three years in prison. Holly's grandparents, now in their seventies and enjoying their retirement years, offered Holly a home but insisted that she obey their rules of no drugs, no alcohol, no cigarettes, and to attend church with them on Sundays. Sarah Collier wanted to bring some structure into Holly's life. They turned the basement of their home into a studio apartment for their granddaughter, which contained a bedroom, living room, and glass patio doors leading out to the lawn. Holly, however, had no intention of going to church or conforming to the rules imposed on her and within a short amount of time, there were almost daily quarrels between Holly and her grandmother.

Sandy, after a quarrel with her father, Tim, and stepmother, Elizabeth, had gone to stay with her mother, Sandra Maddox, in Griffin twenty miles from Fayetteville. The two girls were devastated to be so far apart from each other and wrote to each other daily. Holly, to lessen the pain and loneliness, would chain smoke marijuana and dream of the day she and Sandy could be together all the time. Finally, after a particular nasty quarrel with her grandmother, Holly ran away and made her way to Sandy's mother's house in Griffin. Her grandparents pursued her and brought her back home and forbade her to have any more contact with Sandy.

Sarah Collier knew of her granddaughter's romance with Sandy, and it disgusted her. In addition, she also believed that Sandy was a bad influence on her granddaughter. Holly became angry and began to hate her grandparents, especially her grandmother. Holly felt trapped and began to think about killing them. In a secret meeting with Sandy, Holly told her of her plan to kill her grandparents. Both girls then set out to try and procure a gun by asking friends if anyone knew a way of obtaining one. They believed that with the grandparents out of the way they would be free to be together.

## TEENAGE GIRL KILLERS

On a warm July day, the girls ran away together. They took with them a $50 bag of marijuana and some meth pills and took off. While they were away, the Colliers asked the congregation at their church to pray for their troubled granddaughter. They also reported her missing to the police. Four days later, after running out of drugs and money, the girls returned to their prospective homes. In the state of Georgia, it is against the law to run away and upon Holly's return, there was a court hearing where Holly was warned if she ran away again she would face probation. On leaving the courthouse, Holly was furious and after stubbing a cigarette out on her grandfather's truck, she told them she was going to kill them.

Carl Collier repeated this conversation to his son Kevin and confessed that at times Holly scared him. Kevin later said that he knew his niece was troubled, but he thought the trouble was limited to running away and smoking pot. He now wishes he'd taken the conversation with his father a little more seriously.

Unbeknownst to the Colliers, at night when they had gone to bed, Holly would sneak out to meet Sandy or let Sandy into her basement room. On the night of August the 1$^{st}$, Sandy and Holly were in the basement of the house on Plantation Drive listening to music, making love, and smoking marijuana. At around 2 a.m., they went to visit a friend and spent around three hours smoking joints laced with crack before returning to Plantation Drive.

They spent the following day holed up in the basement chain-smoking joints and disguising the smell with air freshener. When they had smoked nearly all the marijuana, they both wanted more but neither girl had any money. They were both feeling wired and jittery from the crack and needed more marijuana to soften the effects of the come down. Sandy suggested they steal Carl's truck and drive into town to get some more dope. Holly said they would have to kill her grandparents first. The girls looked at each other and in that look reached an agreement. Holly went upstairs to the kitchen and returned with a large carving knife. The two girls then took it in turns to stab the mattress to ensure the knife was sharp enough for their evil intentions.

With a blue pen, Holly wrote a to-do list on her arm:

KEYS. KILL. MONEY. JEWELRY.

They then had to lure the grandparents downstairs. They rolled their last joint, smoked it, and blew the smoke into the air vents knowing that as soon as the grandparents got a whiff of the smell they would come straight down to Holly's room.

Sure enough, they soon heard the footsteps of the grandparents coming down the stairs. Sandy hid, squeezing down into the narrow space between Holly's bed and the wall. Holly hid the knife behind her back as Sarah stood in the doorway with her hands on her hips.

"What's going on in here?" the old lady demanded.

# TEENAGE GIRL KILLERS

Holly closed her eyes, stepped forward, and plunged the knife into her grandmother. The knife punched through the elderly woman's blouse and cut deep into her flesh, the sharp blade passing between her ribs and into her right lung. Her grandfather, after a moment of shocked hesitation, lunged at Holly and punched her on the chin, throwing her back onto her bed. Her grandfather pinned her to the bed and yelled at her,

"You're on drugs! You don't know what you're doing."

Holly called out,

"Sandy! Help me! Help me!"

As Sandy crawled out from her hiding place, Carl Collier raced out of the room and up the stairs.

"Go after him, Holly, quick," shouted Sandy.

Holly gave the carving knife to Sandy and raced after Carl Collier. She found him in the kitchen, with a knife in one hand and the phone in the other. Holly charged towards her grandfather, knocking the knife and phone from his hands. At that moment, Sandy appeared in the kitchen doorway shaking, wild-eyed, and covered in blood. Carl picked up the nearest object within reach, a coffee cup, and flung it at the girls.

Holly picked up the knife she had knocked from her grandfather's hand, pounced on him, and began stabbing him ferociously over and over again in his face, shoulders, and neck before he fell to the floor with blood gushing from his neck where the knife was still embedded.

Holly returned to the basement. At the foot of the stairs lay her grandmother with knife wounds to her head, chest, and neck where Sandy had stabbed her as the old woman had tried to get away. Amazingly, Sarah was still alive. Holly picked up the carving knife lying close to the old woman and stabbed her grandmother again: the 22nd and final fatal wound.

The two blood-soaked girls then did a brief search of the house looking for money and jewelry which they packed into Holly's knapsack, along with a change of clothes and a few other items and the keys to Carl's indigo blue Chevrolet Silverado truck. They squabbled slightly over whether to take the knives with them.

"We've got to. The knives are evidence against us," Holly said as she pulled the knife out of Carl Collier's neck.

The two girls, still dressed in their bloody clothes, hastily clambered into the truck. With Sandy driving, the two girls decided to drive to a friend's house, Sara, in Griffen. They phoned Sara and said they were on their way. When Sara opened the door to her house she was appalled at the sight of her two blood-covered friends. They told her they had been mugged and asked if they could take a shower and clean up. When Holly undressed for her shower, she noticed that there was blood on her underwear, socks, and inside her shoes.

## TEENAGE GIRL KILLERS

While Sandy was taking her shower, Holly told Sara the truth of what they had done. Sara was visibly shocked and asked them to leave her house. Once they had left, Sara found her parents and told them what Holly had told her. Her parents advised her to call the police immediately and tell them. This she did and the police, after taking Sara's details, said they would investigate.

Following the call, the police immediately sent officers to the Colliers' home to investigate. Having no reply to their ringing of the doorbell, the police broke in and discovered the brutal bloody scene. Lt. Col. Bruce Jordan, Fayette County's chief investigator, was immediately called. They found 75-year-old Carl in the kitchen with fifteen stab wounds to his body and 73-year-old Sarah at the bottom of the basement stairs with twenty-two stab wounds. Bruce Jordan later said that the Collier house was,

"The bloodiest scene I've worked in 25 years on the force."

In Holly's room, the lingering smell of marijuana hung in the air of the bloody wall-soaked room. In the room, detectives found a poem written by Holly. It described how unhappy she had been and how she would cry herself to sleep and another line of the poem read,

*"All I want to do is kill."*

An arrest warrant was issued for Holly and Sandy, and Bruce Jordan alerted the U.S. Marshalls to find the girls and the stolen truck.

# HOLLY HARVEY AND SANDRA KETCHUM

*Carl and Sarah Collier*

Sandy and Holly, chain-smoking continuously and with the bloody knives still in their possession, decided to drive to Tybee Island on the Georgia coast near the city of Savannah. Tybee Island was a popular tourist destination, rich in history and natural beauty, and a three-to-four-hour drive from Fayetteville. On the drive, Holly called several friends from her cell phone and urged them to watch the 10 O'clock news.

It was late evening when the girls arrived on Tybee Island. They parked the truck in a parking lot of a nursing home and then strolled down to the beach. They spotted two boys, Brian Clayton age 22, and his younger brother, Brent age 14, sitting on the beach smoking cigarettes. Holly and Sandy had run out of cigarettes, so Sandy approached the boys and asked if they would let her and her

# TEENAGE GIRL KILLERS

friend have one. The boys happily obliged and invited the girls to sit down and join them.

The girls sat down and introduced themselves as Jessica and Casey. The four of them began chatting as the Atlantic Ocean breeze rustled their hair. Brent told them that they had arrived on Tybee Island that day where their parents had bought a beach house. Sandy confessed to Brian that they were runaways and had nowhere to stay that night. Brian said they could stay at the beach house that night if it was okay with his mother. He called his mother on his cell phone, who said that the girls could sleep on a mattress in an unused back bedroom. That night, Holly and Sandy, after a long and eventful day, fell asleep wrapped in each other's arms.

Meanwhile back in Fayetteville, the U.S. Marshals, using GPS technology, had tracked Holly's cell phone to Tybee Island but when Holly had climbed out of the truck to walk on the beach she had turned it off, and the signal was lost.

Early the following morning, U.S. Marshalls wandered the streets of the coastal town hoping to find something. They were in luck. At 9 a.m., they found the stolen truck parked at the Oceanside Nursing Center close to the beach, but there was no sign of the girls.

The girls were waking up in the back bedroom of the beach house. Holly switched on her phone to see if there were any messages. That was all the U.S. Marshalls needed to pin the girls down. Twenty-five armed police officers surrounded the beach house as the Clayton family was settling down to breakfast. When the doorbell rang, Brian went to answer it and was startled to find an armed detective flashing his card at him. It was Lt. Col. Bruce Jordan who asked him if he had two teenage girls in the house. Brian indicated the way to the back bedroom. It was over in seconds; Holly and Sandy were pinned to the floor by the police, arrested, and handcuffed. In Sandy's pockets were two knives. and on Holly's arm, slightly faded but still legible, was her "to do" list: kill, keys, money, jewelry.

The Clayton family was in complete shock as Holly and Sandy were arrested for the murders of Carl and Sarah Collier. Bruce Jordan, in his report of the arrest, stated that Holly acted "callously and cockily," and Sandy Ketchum had shown regret for what she had done and had told officers that she would cooperate fully. Later in the police station, Sandy made a full statement detailing the crime to Bruce Jordan and agreed to testify against Holly.

On August 5, 2004, the two teenagers appeared before a Fayette County magistrate to hear the charges filed against them. Holly and Sandy were charged as adults with two felony counts of murder and two counts of malice murder. Both girls cried as if they finally realized the horror of their crimes. Under Georgia state law, the death penalty did not apply to them because they were under 17 years of age, but they were facing a maximum sentence of life in prison without parole. Holly and Sandy were detained in separate detention centers. A local newspaper reporting on the case nicknamed them as,

"Teenage Thelma and Louise."

The girls never went to trial as they both made plea agreements. As part of Holly's plea agreement, she had to give a detailed description of the crime to the judge. For half an hour, Holly spoke quietly and choked back sobs as she recounted the day of the murders in the Fayette County Superior Court to Judge Pascal English. Judge English asked what she thought should happen to her. Holly replied,

"I think I should be dead."

The judge muttered under his breath,

"We both agree on that."

On Thursday, April 14, 2005, Judge Pascal English sentenced Holly to two life sentences for the two murders. She will be eligible for parole after serving twenty years.

Sandy Ketchum, in return for her cooperation with the authorities, was sentenced to life for murder and armed robbery and could be eligible for parole after serving ten years. Both girls are detained in separate prisons.

Outside the courthouse, after sentencing, Tim Ketchum, Sandy's father said,

"I didn't raise her to be that type of person. I want to say to the community I'm very sorry this happened."

## HOLLY HARVEY AND SANDRA KETCHUM

Holly's mother, Carla, said in a statement from prison,

"I've lost three people whom I love."

Kevin Collier, Holly's uncle, said of his parents,

"I'm sure they hoped they would get Holly to turn her life around. They obviously didn't expect this to be their payment."

*HOLLY HARVEY and SANDRA KETCHUM*

# CHELSEA O' MAHONEY

Chelsea Kayleigh Peaches O'Mahoney entered the world on November 15, 1989 in a London hospital. Her mother, Suzanne Cato, was a heroin addict and heavy drinker and her father is unknown. Her early life with her mother in South London left a lot to be desired. On a few occasions, Chelsea was found wandering alone on the streets of south London late at night.

At the age of seven, Chelsea went to live with her aunt June O'Mahoney. June lived in a ground-floor flat of Sambrook House tower block on a rough, crime-ridden, social housing estate in Kennington, South London. It was an estate overcrowded amid high rates of unemployment and poverty where residents lived in fear with muggings happening daily and where teenage gangs skulked around the dirty alleyways after dark.

This was the neighborhood that Chelsea grew up in and made friends with the other kids on the estate. By the time, she was thirteen she had become part of a gang. They would play games of dare, bully other kids, knock a football about, and fight with rival

## CHELSEA O'MAHONEY

gangs.

In 2004, Chelsea's gang began attacking vulnerable people for fun. On the evening of the 29th of October, the gang decided that the following night they would go "Happy Slapping," and beat up some tramps, druggies, or just random people on the street.

"Happy Slapping," was a fad that, in 2004, was gaining popularity with teenage street gangs in England. These gangs would randomly attack people and record the attack on mobile phones which would be then circulated amongst their friends.

Late the following night of October the 30th, four members of the gang met up: Reece Sargeant, age 21, Darren Case, age 18, David Blenman, age 17, and Chelsea then age 14. In an hour of mindless violence, they attacked eight people on London's South Bank and caused the death of David Morley.

David Morley had five years previously survived a nail bomb attack at the gay bar in which he worked, the Admiral Duncan in London's Soho; this was one of the three nail bomb attacks carried out in London by Neo-Nazi David Copeland.

At around 3.00a.m. in the morning, the gang of four approached David, age 37, and his companion Alastair Whiteside who were sitting on a street bench close to London's Hungerford Bridge. The gang started to beat the two men up. As Reece, Darren, and David punched and kicked the two men, Chelsea stood by laughing and filming the attack on her NEC mobile phone. At one point, according to Alastair who survived the attack, Chelsea called out,

"We're doing a documentary on happy slapping - pose for the camera."

Alistair also related how when David was lying on the ground barely conscious, Chelsea went up to David and kicked him two or three times in the head, "like a football."

The gang then left the men lying on the pavement and went on to attack three more victims.

A passerby who discovered the two men called for an ambulance and the two men were taken to St. Thomas' Hospital, Lambeth, Despite every effort by doctors, David Morley died a few hours after arriving at the hospital. A post-mortem examination found he had suffered forty-four injuries, including five fractured ribs and a ruptured spleen.

The last attack of the night was on a homeless man, Wayne Miller, who survived. It was filmed on CCTV camera. With the video footage and statements from the seven surviving victims, the police soon identified the gang of four.

On searching Chelsea's bedroom at the time of her arrest, the police found a hidden diary full of depraved descriptions of beatings she and her gang had meted out to random strangers in South London. Chelsea was arrested and held at the juvenile Oakhill secure

## CHELSEA O'MAHONEY

unit in Milton Keynes, just north of London, to await trial at the old Bailey. While there, Chelsea was several times involved in incidents of violence, one of which involved hurling a television set against a wall.

The gang of four went on trial at London's Old Bailey court in January of 2006 for the murder of David Morley and for grievous bodily harm (GBH) to others. The prosecution showed the jury the graphic CCTV footage of the gang's final attack of the night, on a homeless man sleeping in a doorway near London's Waterloo Station. Chelsea could be seen holding her mobile phone in the air, filming the violence. All four could be seen repeatedly kicking the victim, Wayne Miller, in the head before rushing off "whooping" in delight.

*CHELSEA O'MAHONEY*

# TEENAGE GIRL KILLERS

The jury returned a verdict of manslaughter and grievous bodily harm against the four defendants. The judge on sentencing said:

"You are all old enough to understand the realities and the consequences of your actions. You sought enjoyment from humiliation and pleasure from the infliction of pain. You called this 'happy slapping'; no victim on the receiving end would dignify it with such a deceptive description."

He continued by saying that the gang had filmed their assaults for "amusement," "gratification," and "enhanced status."

Chelsea O'Mahoney was sentenced to eight years, presumably perceived as less culpable due to her age. She was released on parole after four years.

Reece Sargeant, Darren Case, and David Blenman were sentenced to twelve years in prison.

# CINDY COLLIER AND SHIRLEY WOLF

**SHIRLEY WOLF**

Shirley Wolf was born in Brooklyn, New York in 1969 to Louis James and Katherine Wolf. She was eldest of four and the only daughter. Her father was a carpenter by trade. When Shirley was six, her father had a disabling accident that prevented him from working. In 1976, when Shirley was seven, the family moved to Placerville, California, a historic community from the gold-rush days, twenty-eight miles from Auburn.

Louis James began sexually abusing his daughter Shirley when she was just three-years-old. Occasionally, she was also abused by her father's brother and her paternal grandfather. When she was nine, her father raped her in the family bathroom. Over the following five years, Louis James continually raped her and when she entered puberty, he bought her birth control pills.

Finally, Shirley told her mother, Katherine. Her mother believed her as she had once seen him sexually abusing Shirley when she was three. Katherine and Shirley went to the police. Louis James was subsequently arrested and in a plea bargain pled guilty to a lesser charge of child molestation. Consequently, he only spent 100 days in the local county jail before been released on probation. When Louis James returned home, because he was a registered sex offender, he was forbidden contact with his daughter. Shirley was removed to two different foster homes before being sent to a Sacramento group home. She was desperately unhappy and missed her family. She begged to go home, repeatedly ran away from the group home, and began fighting in school.

### CINDY COLLIER

Cindy Collier was born in 1968 to David Lee and Betty Avery Collier. They divorced when Cindy was one. Her mother remarried but that marriage also ended in a divorce. Betty Avery then began to work as a waitress to support her daughter and three sons. With their mother out working long hours, the children were left to fend for themselves for hours at a time.

By the age of twelve, Cindy was in trouble with the police. By the time she was fifteen, she had a criminal record for assault, burglary, drug use, and theft. At her local Juvenile Hall, she was known by the staff as "assaultive," and for possessing a fierce temper.

At the age of fifteen, Cindy was 5'9", weighed nearly 140 pounds, and had brown eyes that radiated fierce hostility making her a formidable physical presence. At her school in Auburn, Chana High, she was known as a bully. David Silva, a former classmate,

said,

"If she took a dislike to someone she would yell at them and push them around."

*Cindy Collier*

## CINDY AND SHIRLEY MEET

When Cindy Collier and Shirley Wolf met on Tuesday, June 14, 1983, they immediately struck up a bond, discovering in each other a kindred spirit. Within hours of meeting, they were off creating mayhem in a condominium development mainly inhabited by the elderly that Shirley Collier's grandparents used to live in. They wanted to steal a car and take it for a drive, but they would have to get hold of some car keys. They began knocking on random doors in the condominium trying to gain entrance by asking for a glass of water or to use the phone or pretending to seek directions.

# TEENAGE GIRL KILLERS

Most of the residents refused to open their doors to the wicked looking girls. However, eighty-five-year-old Anna Brackett, a retired seamstress with great-grandchildren of Shirley's and Cindy's age, invited them in when they knocked on her door asking for a glass of water. Anna Brackett sat them in her neat living room of her two-bedroom condo and began chatting with the girls. After about an hour, she received a phone call from her son Carl to say he was on his way to pick her up and take her to Bingo.

*Shirley Wolf*

The girls realized if they wanted her car keys they had to act quickly. Shirley Wolf jumped up out of her chair, grabbed Anna Brackett by the throat, and threw her to the floor. Cindy ran to the kitchen and seized a butcher's knife and handed it to Shirley. Shirley began stabbing the elderly woman repeatedly. Anna was begging her to stop. She said,

## CINDY COLLIER AND SHIRLEY WOLF

"You are killing me."

Shirley replied,

"Good."

When the girls were sure Anna was dead, they ransacked the condominium for any jewelry or money and the car keys to the 1970 Dodge parked outside. Before leaving, they ripped the telephone from the wall and then hurriedly left the apartment. Anna Brackett's car refused to start and so the girls fled the complex on foot, minutes before Carl Brackett and his wife pulled up outside his mother's condominium.

When Carl and his wife entered his mother's condominium, they were met with the grisly bloody scene. Carl later said,

"It was like a scene from the film Psycho."

Placer County sheriff's officers and an ambulance were quickly on the scene and began to make house-to-house inquiries. The officers were given reports and descriptions of two suspicions teenage girls who had been hanging around the complex. A couple of neighbors had recognized one as being Cindy Collier, having remembered her from when her grandparents lived in the community.

The detective in charge of the investigation, George Coelho, did not think that two young girls would be capable of committing such a frenzied attack but decided they ought to talk to Cindy, if only to eliminate her from their inquiries. Her address was on record, so they proceeded, even though late at night, to her home she lived in with foster parents. The detectives were in luck as not only was Cindy there, but Shirley was there as well.

When confronted by the detectives, Shirley Wolf confessed within minutes. The girls were arrested and before the detectives had time to read them their Miranda Rights, Cindy recited the Miranda warning to them. They were taken downtown to the police station for further questioning. Shirley told the detectives in a tape-recorded confession,

"We decided we were going to kill her when we saw her. She was just an old lady. Just a perfect setup. We killed her because we wanted her car, and we didn't want to get caught."

Further on in the statement she said,

"We both felt excited. I had done something I had never done before."

Detectives, on searching through Shirley's possessions, found a notebook she used as a diary. On Tuesday, June 14, in barely legible writing she had written,

"Today, Cindy and I ran away and killed an old lady. It was lots of fun."

In Cindy's tape recorded interview, she said,

"To honestly tell you the truth, we didn't feel any badness.

Then after we did it, we wanted to do another one. We just wanted to kill someone. Just for fun."

Cindy also revealed to detectives that she had been raped by a family member and by another man in Tahoe, who then threw her down a flight of concrete stairs.

"My childhood has been rotten. I've been beaten since I was born. I have tried to kill myself before and all it did was bring frustrations, so I take it out on others. I don't like them because they probably think they're better than I am. I do not want them around. I want them to pay."

She also bragged to detectives,

"I have hurt people, I have stabbed people, I have shot people. I've thrown people off the Auburn Dam."

Detectives then asked if she had ever killed anyone before. Cindy replied,

"No. But I've tried so many times."

On July 29, 1983, Cindy and Shirley were tried under state law as juveniles. They were both found guilty of first-degree murder and sentenced to the maximum sentence allowed for minors. Both girls, when convicted, appeared remorseless and almost bored.

Cindy's father, David Lee Collier, reappeared in her life for a short time after her arrest and visited her while incarcerated in Juvenile Hall but disappeared out of her life again before the trial.

Her mother did not attend any of the court hearings.

Following the conclusion of the trial, Shirley Wolf's court-appointed lawyer, Thomas Condit, said,

"I'd like to say that Shirley felt sorry, but I can't. That is part of her problem. She told me that while she was killing the old lady, she was thinking of everybody she hated—her father and her grandmother, but her psychiatrist believes it was a symbolic killing of her own mother."

## WHAT HAPPENED TO CINDY AND SHIRLEY?

Cindy Collier spent nine years in the California Youth Authority facility in Ventura. She obtained her junior college degree and then went on to study law under the tutelage of lawyers from Pepperdine University School of Law. Cindy was paroled on August 20, 1992. She is married and has four children. She lives in northern California and leads a criminal free life.

Shirley Wolf was incarcerated for twelve years. Her last year was spent at the massive Central California Women's Facility near Chowchilla. During her time imprisoned, she completed her high school education and turned to God. Her family neither wrote nor visited her.

On June 30, 1995, just over twelve years after the murder of Anna Brackett, Shirley was granted her freedom from prison. Since that day, she has been arrested on numerous occasions for crimes ranging from assault to prostitution.

# ALYSSA BUSTAMANTE

Alyssa Bustamante was born on January 28, 1994 in California. Her parents, Ceaser and Michelle Bustamante, were cousins by marriage. At the time that Michelle gave birth to Alyssa, she was only fifteen-years-old. Both Ceaser and Michelle were meth and marijuana users and drifted around the state of California before moving to St. Martins, a rural town just west of Jefferson City, Missouri in 1996 which is where Michelle's mother Karen Brooke lived.

When Alyssa was six, her mother gave birth to twin boys and a couple of years later she gave birth to another daughter. As Alyssa grew up, she witnessed both her parents' drug habits and the physical abuse of her mother by her father. Her father was arrested and convicted of felony assault and sentenced to prison for three concurrent long terms in the Missouri Eastern Correctional Facility. Her mother Michelle struggled to pay the rent and landed herself three misdemeanor criminal convictions for drunken driving and possession of marijuana. As Michelle struggled, her drug and alcohol addictions worsened.

# ALYSSA BUSTAMANTE

In 2002, Karen Brooke, the children's grandmother, was given legal guardianship of Alyssa and her three younger siblings. The children moved into the grandparents' house, a ranch-style dwelling at 626 Lomo Drive, St Martins. It was a house surrounded by lots of open space and woods for the children in which they could play.

As Alyssa slipped into her teen years, she began having psychological issues. She suffered from severe depression and on Monday, the 3rd of September of 2007 she attempted suicide by swallowing a bottle of Tylenol pills and was hospitalized. She had also cut herself hundreds of times and carved the words "hate" and "pain" into her arms. While in the hospital, she was prescribed Prozac. She was in the hospital for two weeks.

Upon her release, Alyssa was admitted to the outpatient program of the Pathways Mental Health Center in Jefferson City. During her time as a patient at the clinic, between 2007 and 2009, she was treated by no less than three different therapists. The clinic continued to prescribe her Prozac.

Teens cutting themselves is more common than one might think. According to one United States psychiatric study, a third to a half of teenagers aged between the ages of twelve and eighteen engage in self-injury at least once. Destructive as this behavior is, most of the teens — about 60% — aren't trying to end their lives, which is why psychiatrists call it non-suicidal self-injury (NSSI)?

"The majority of the teens want to kill their emotional angst," according to Janis Whitlock, PhD, director of Cornell University's Research Program on Self-Injurious Behavior.

Experts aren't entirely sure why the action of inflicting physical hurt helps, but self-injurers say they feel more relaxed afterward as if exchanging inner angst for the powerful physical sensation. Others, who are emotionally frozen, may just want to prove they're capable of experiencing anything at all. Brain chemistry also plays a part — cutting releases endorphins, resulting in a numbing or pleasurable sensation.

"Self-injury is a form of self-medication," says Janis Whitlock.

Though professionals fall short of calling the behavior a true addiction, it can be compulsive: The more a person cuts, the more he/she'll crave this relief when tension builds. Over time, the urge becomes impossible to resist.

People who cut or self-injure sometimes have other mental health problems that contribute to their emotional tension. Cutting is sometimes (but not always) associated with depression, bipolar disorder, eating disorders, obsessive thinking, or compulsive behaviors. It can also be a sign of mental health problems that cause people to have trouble controlling their impulses or to take unnecessary risks.

# ALYSSA BUSTAMANTE

Like other teenagers at Jefferson City High School, which Alyssa attended and was ranked as being in the top third of her class, she was deeply involved with social media on the internet and had pages on Facebook, Myspace, and Twitter. She also had a YouTube account where she would post video clips of herself and sometimes her twin brothers. Alyssa also attended the Jefferson City Mormon church with her grandparents and participated at various youth groups and activities at the church. Alyssa began to be thought of amongst her peers as a "Goth." She began to only dress in black and painted her eyes with heavy black eyeliner.

Karen Brooke was worried about her grand-daughter. Despite all the counseling, therapists, and medication Alyssa was still cutting herself. At the beginning of October 2009, the clinic raised her dose of Prozac to 40 milligrams a day, the highest she had ever been prescribed.

Karen later said this seemed to have a detrimental effect on her granddaughter. Alyssa stopped coming straight home from school and missed the family evening meals. Karen telephoned Alyssa's doctor and was told that the higher dose would take about a month to level out.

On the early evening of October 21, 2009, a nine-year-old girl, Elizabeth Olten, a friend of Emma, Alyssa's six-year-old sister, who lived four doors away, failed to return home from playing at the

## TEENAGE GIRL KILLERS

Brook's home. When darkness had fallen at 7 p.m. and she still failed to return home, Elizabeth's parents contacted the police.

An extensive search was launched in the woods lying at the back of the Brook's and Olten's homes. The search team consisted of hundreds of local volunteers, over one-hundred law enforcement officers, dogs, emergency workers, and local officials. A helicopter equipped with infrared detection devices was utilized with the search on the first night. The search the first night was in difficult conditions, it was cold and raining heavily. The search was eventually called off and begun again the following morning at daybreak.

The police, at this point, feared that the little girl had been kidnapped as she made her way home alone through the woods. As the search continued, detectives began to make house to house inquiries. All of the Brook's family were interviewed and Alyssa supposedly suggested to an FBI officer that Elizabeth had probably been kidnapped and that whoever had done so deserved to be convicted.

As the search continued, officers found a hole in the ground dug in the shape of a shallow grave just behind the Brook's home. A friend of Alyssa's confided in the detectives that Alyssa had told her that she wanted to know what committing a murder would be like.

On the 23rd of October, detectives again interviewed Alyssa. They asked her about the shallow grave they had found in the woods. She admitted she had dug it saying she like digging holes in the woods. Under more intense questioning, Alyssa finally confessed to having killed Elizabeth.

Alyssa then took them to the spot she had buried Elizabeth. She had buried her in a hole, covered with five to six inches of soil on top, and then covered with leaves. She admitted she had dug the two graves the week before. Detectives wondered for whom the other had been intended.

Alyssa was arrested and taken into custody. As news of her arrest spread, the small community was in deep shock.

The autopsy revealed that Elizabeth had been strangled, stabbed, and her throat and wrists had been slashed. Alyssa confessed she had lured Elizabeth into the woods by offering to walk her home through the woods, and saving Elizabeth the longer walk by road.

Elizabeth Olten was buried a few days later. A horse-drawn carriage carried her casket to the cemetery, where her family and friends wore her favorite color: pink.

Meanwhile the detectives who had searched Alyssa's bedroom found some chilling discoveries. In a diary written a week before the murder, Alyssa had written complaining that her phone battery was dead, so she couldn't call anyone about the depression and rage she was feeling. She wrote,

"If I don't talk about it, I bottle it up and when I explode, someone's going to die."

In an entry written on the evening of October 21st she had written,

"I just fucking killed someone. I strangled them and slit their throat and stabbed them now they're dead. I don't know how to feel atm [at the moment]."

Later Alyssa wrote,

"It was amazing. As soon as you get over the 'ohmygawd I can't do this' feeling, it's pretty enjoyable. I'm kinda nervous and shaky though right now. Kay, I gotta go to church now...lol."

Alyssa had then attended her church for a youth dance while the search was underway for Elizabeth.

The detectives then took a look at Alyssa's social media accounts. On her twitter account a few weeks prior to the murder she had tweeted,

"This is all I want in life; a reason for all this pain."

On another tweet, she had written that she was,

"Somewhere I don't want to be."

On YouTube she had an account in the name of OkamiKage (Japanese for "WolfShadow.") Her hobbies she listed as "killing people and cutting." On the site, she showed a home video of her

brother's. Before the clip she wrote,

"This is where it gets good; this is where my brothers get hurt."

In the clip, she eggs on her twin brothers to touch an electrified cattle fence, well aware of the pain it would cause them before doing so herself.

On her Facebook profile, she had photos of her slashed wrists and another photo of herself pointing a finger at her head like a gun with smeared lipstick around her mouth resembling blood.

Alyssa made her first court appearance on the 18th of November 2009, shackled and dressed in a prison jumpsuit of lime green. She was charged with First Degree Murder and because of the knife, armed criminal action. She entered a plea of "Not Guilty," as advised by her lawyer. As Alyssa had only just turned fifteen at the time of the murder the judge had to decide if she was to be tried as a juvenile or an adult, which could have made her eligible for the death penalty. The judge listened to arguments from the prosecution and defense lawyers. The judge decided that she should be tried as an adult.

Her defense attorney, following the judge's decision, expressed disappointment and said,

"We are throwing away the child, and we are signing a death sentence for Alyssa. She is not going to survive her time in the Cole County jail."

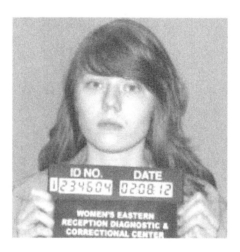

Following the decision, it was reported that Alyssa had tried to harm herself by cutting herself with her own fingernails and was showing signs of extreme anxiety and severe depression in jail. Her attorney filed a motion to the judge to have her removed immediately to receive immediate psychiatric treatment at a mental institution. The motion was granted, and Alyssa was moved to Hawthorn Children's Psychiatric Hospital. Later, the judge ordered her to be taken to the Fulton State Hospital for a psychiatric evaluation.

A trial start date of May 16th, 2011 had been set for Alyssa where she would stand trial charged as an adult with first-degree murder. However, after further delays, Alyssa's trial did not begin until January 30th, 2012. After a plea agreement, she agreed to plead guilty to a lesser charge of 2nd degree murder, thereby escaping the possibility of the death penalty or life without the possibility of parole. The punishment for murder in the second degree can be life with the possibility of parole or 10-30 years. The sentence for armed criminal action is three years to life. By pleading guilty, she also freed herself from trial by jury. The purpose of the January 30th hearing was to determine the length of her sentence.

After Alyssa pleaded guilty, Judge Patricia Joyce Cole asked Alyssa to describe her actions on October 21, 2009. Alyssa stated,

"I strangled her and stabbed her in the chest."

The judge then asked if she had also cut Elizabeth Olten's throat. Alyssa responded,

"Yes."

The prosecutor, Mark Richardson, wanted Alyssa to have a life in prison and seventy-one years for the life Elizabeth had lost. He told the court she was a thrill killer who showed no remorse. It was evident, he argued, that she had planned the murder in advance by digging two graves in a nearby wooded area. He continued by saying that Alyssa then went on with her life as usual: attending school and hanging out with friends; all the while waiting for the perfect opportunity to murder. He called Sergeant David Rice to the witness box who testified that Alyssa told him,

"She wanted to know what it felt like to kill someone."

Mark Richardson continued,

"She committed the murder after deliberation, which means cold deliberation or cold reflection on the matter for any length of time."

Mark Richardson then read out selected writings from Alyssa's diary and her YouTube profile to prove her premeditated plans for murder.

Patty Preiss, Elizabeth's mother, described how she had told her daughter to be back for dinner at 6p.m. but never saw her again. She also said through tears,

"So much has been lost at the hands of this evil monster. Elizabeth was given a death sentence, and we were given a life sentence."

When talking about Alyssa, Patty said,

"I hate her, I hate everything about her," and described her as "not even human." She asked the judge to consider the case as if it were her child who had been murdered.

Alyssa's defense lawyers argued for a sentence of less than life in prison. Her defense lawyer, Donald Catlett, recounted Alyssa's early family history of drug abuse and unstable upbringing: that her father was in prison and her mother, due to her drug and alcohol abuse problems, had abandoned her.

Psychologists for the defense team testified that Alyssa was "severely emotionally disturbed" and "psychologically damaged." They said that she suffered from Major Depression and displayed symptoms of Borderline Personality Disorder. They gave details of her suicide attempts and her history of self-harm.

Ron Wilson, from the Pathways Mental Health Clinic who initially treated Alyssa in 2007, testified that Alyssa only harmed herself and had no prior history of hurting others.

Psychologist Dr. Rosalyn Schultz testified that the treatment Alyssa was getting at the Pathways Mental Health Clinic was inadequate. She said that as Alyssa was suicidal she should have been treated as an inpatient. Dr. Rosalyn Schultz went on to say that there was a link between suicide and homicide and that homicide is externalizing the actions of suicide. She said that if Alyssa had received better care and better treatment it would have made a difference in her progress.

Psychiatrist Dr. Edwin Johnstone said that the medication Alyssa was on, Prozac, could lead to greater instances of violence, particularly in adolescents, teenagers, and females who were most at risk of the side effects of the drug. The side effects could include agitation, irritability, impulsiveness, insomnia, suicide, and violent events. He testified that the higher dosage she had been prescribed two-weeks before the crime could have increased Alyssa's mood swings and violent tendencies, as her diary entries following the increased dosage had become increasingly violent. In his opinion, Prozac was "a major contributing factor" in Alyssa's crime. He testified that people who were prescribed Prozac "were showing an abundance of suicides and violent events, including homicides."

A prosecution psychiatrist witness, Dr. Anthony Rothschild, claimed that there was no scientific evidence of Prozac causing homicides or even increasing aggression. He said it had been proven to decrease hostility and anger in people suffering from major depression and borderline personality disorders.

Karen Brooke, Alyssa's grandmother, described to the court

the two year struggle she had had trying to get the right treatment for Alyssa and described the ups and down of Alyssa's moods and behaviors and how within a week of the increased dosage of Prozac Alyssa's behavior had deteriorated.

At the end of all the arguments presented by the defense and prosecution, the judge adjourned the court to the following day for the sentencing. As the judge announced this, Eizabeth Olten's grandmother, Sandy Corn, yelled out,

"I think Alyssa should get out of jail the same day Elizabeth gets out of the grave!"

**END GAME**

Before passing down the sentence on February 8th, 2012, Judge Pat Joyce asked Alyssa, now age 18, if she had anything she wished to say. Alyssa nodded her head and stood up with her feet shackled together and her hands shackled to her waist and faced Elizabeth Olsen's family who sat silently.

"I know words can never be enough, and they can never adequately describe how horribly I feel for all of this," Alyssa said in a faltering voice. "If I could give my life to get her back I would. I just want to say I'm sorry for what happened. I'm so sorry."

Judge Pat Joyce then sentenced Alyssa to life in prison on the 2nd degree murder charge, with the possibility of parole, and thirty years for armed criminal action, to be served consecutively.

Alyssa was then taken out of court and driven to Cole County Jail to begin her life sentence from which she may be paroled in thirty-five years, at the age of fifty-three.

The simple explanation given by Alyssa herself was that she wanted to know what it felt like to kill someone. The psychological implications of that statement are obvious: normal, mentally stable people, even if they have ever pondered that question to themselves, do not go and actually commit a murder in order to find out.

# PROZAC

It would appear to most people that Alyssa was a very disturbed child who did not get the psychiatric help and care she needed. If you search on the internet for Prozac you can find sites with warnings about the side effects of Prozac on young people under the age of twenty-five.

In Winnipeg, Canada in September of 2011, a judge ruled that a Winnipeg teenager was driven to commit an unprovoked murder because of the adverse affects of taking Prozac. The defense lawyer in the case had told the court that the teenager's parents had complained to his doctor that his behavior was getting worse while taking the drug, which prompted his doctor to raise the dosage.

"He had become irritable, restless, agitated, aggressive, and unclear in his thinking," the judge said. "It was while in that state he overreacted in an impulsive, explosive, and violent way. Now that his body and mind are free and clear of any effects of Prozac, he is simply not the same youth in behavior or character."

The manufacturer's warning for Prozac states under Adverse

# TEENAGE GIRL KILLERS

Reactions:

"Nervous System - frequent: abnormal dreams and agitation; - infrequent: abnormal gait, acute brain syndrome, akathisia, amnesia, apathy, ... delusions, depersonalization, euphoria, hallucinations, hostility, ... manic reaction, paranoid reaction, psychosis, and vertigo; rare: abnormal electroencephalogram, anti-social reaction, chronic brain syndrome .... hysteria..."

According to medical literature, the side effect of "akathisia" is a drug-induced insanity with bizarre and frightening characteristics including aggression, anger, hallucinations, self-destructive outbursts, terror, hatred, hostility, and rage.

Anyone who is taking Prozac should be informed that aggression and violence are possible results of using the drug.

Hundreds of lawsuits have been filed against the manufacturer of Prozac for the drug's link to suicide and violent behavior.

In clinical studies conducted, it was found that for children and young adults (24 and under) who take Prozac or similar anti-depressants there was a two-fold increase in suicidal thoughts and behavior compared to those on the placebo. With this finding, the FDA mandated that a black box warning be used for Prozac as well as for other antidepressants. The black box warning is the most serious level of warning available.

# PROZAC

Some prominent lawsuits involving Prozac are:

•The first prominent Prozac lawsuit was settled in 1994 when Prozac user Joseph Wesbecker engaged in a violent workplace shooting spree and killed eight people and injured 12 before committing suicide in 1989. He had been taking Prozac for four weeks before the incident. This Prozac lawsuit claimed that the drug influenced the man to violence; the Prozac lawsuits alleged that the drug posed a major effect on the man and ultimately led him to murder and suicide.

•In 1997, Patricia Williamson of Texas stabbed herself to death in her bathtub. She had begun taking Prozac six days earlier for depression. An out-of-court settlement was made with Eli Lilly.

•In 1996, Reginald Payne, a teacher from Cornwall, killed his wife and threw himself off a cliff. He had been taking Prozac for just 11 days. His family filed a lawsuit against the manufacturing company of Prozac.

•Eli Lilly, the manufacturer of Prozac, has settled hundreds of Prozac litigation cases for as little as $50 million, which is about the profits Prozac sales make in one week.

What is tragic about this case is that if Alyssa had had proper care and treatment, two young lives could have been saved.

# NURSES WHO MURDER

Since ancient Greek times, the *Hippocratic Oath* has been a vow sworn by doctors in which they swear to practice medicine ethically. Nurses do not take the *Hippocratic Oath* but at graduation from nursing school they normally take a vow to do their best for their patients. Frequently called the *Florence Nightingale Vow* it is an adaption of the *Hippocratic Oath*. The vow contains the mantra of "do not harm." The vow has been updated over time, but the same sentiment remains.

This book contains some cases of serial killers, all of whom were female nurses. The crimes of these nurses are heinous and shocking.

Why, one might well ask, would someone who had worked and studied hard to be a nurse, want to harm or injure her patients? The unfortunate truth is that a few people become nurses not to aid others but to have attention, control, or power. If they decide to injure or kill patients, the methods are readily available. They have easy accessibility to patients that are frequently very ill, very young, or very old — and available drugs that are strong enough to kill inconspicuously through an intravenous tube. Murder of patients is about ultimate power: the power of life over death.

Murder is not an act that sits comfortably with the normal image of nurses or care-givers. Nurses are normally wholly trusted by the communities in which they serve. Hospitals are seen as places of care, nurture, and safe harbor. A common reaction of both the public and other medical professionals when confronted with nurses killing patients is to categorize them as "mad".

Luckily, nurses who murder their patients are the exception. They are not the rule. However, the number of cases of nurses accused and convicted of murdering patients is rising. It's almost enough to give you a phobia about going into the hospital!!

# MARIE JEANNERET

Marie Jeanneret entered the world in 1836 to middle class parents in Neuchatel, Switzerland. While an infant, her parents died. A guardian, an uncle, brought her up religiously and ensured that she was well-educated.

*Neuchatel, Switzerland*

# MARIE JEANNERET

As a young lady, she was vain, strong willed, a liar, enjoyed intrigue, and attracting attention. Her interest lay in reading medical books, and she harbored an ambition to become a nurse. She often made visits to doctors complaining of various symptoms, possibly to further her medical knowledge.

During one consultation with a doctor in 1865, she complained about her eyes and even went so far as to pretend to be blind. The consulting doctor thought the affliction imaginary. Another Doctor who she visited prescribed belladonna (deadly nightshade). This enabled her to a lifetime supply of this drug whenever she desired. Belladonna is prescribed as a treatment of individuals with eye infections in whom the symptoms may suddenly appear without warning.

In 1886, Marie Jeanneret became great friends with a Mademoiselle Berthet. They took short breaks together staying in pensions. One evening after dinner, Marie Jeanneret offered Mademoiselle Berthet a mixture of *eau sucre* and wine. Not long afterward, Mademoiselle Berthet was sick and complained about her heart feeling like lead. The following day, Mademoiselle Berthet felt better. Later that evening, Marie Jeanneret made another drink for her friend. That night and all of the following day, Mademoiselle Berthet was delirious. The concerned pension owners sent a telegram to Mademoiselle Berthet's relatives who came and took her home. Upon questioning by her family doctor, Dr. Lamibassy, about her symptoms, he said that he thought she was suffering from belladonna poisoning. The pupils of her eyes were extremely dilated, and her facial features altered. Many months passed before her eyesight became fully restored.

In the 16$^{th}$ and 17$^{th}$ centuries, belladonna drops were often put in the eyes to dilate the pupils to give ladies a wide-eyed innocent look. They may have looked more attractive, but the drops caused them not to be able to focus properly, and they would only have a hazy view with whom they were talking.

Mademoiselle Berthet thought and felt like she had indeed been poisoned but surely only by mistake. She could not believe her friend Marie would do that to her deliberately. What could Marie possibly have to gain from poisoning her?

Marie, shortly after this episode, enrolled at a nursing school in Lausanne. She only remained at the school for two months giving the excuse that her eyes made it impossible for her to work. Occasionally at the nursing school, they obliged her to nurse patients in their own homes. One of the patients she attended to was Madame Chabolz.

When Madame Chabolz's married daughter Madame Eichenberg called on her mother, she found "a face showing intense terror with enormous open eyes, laughing deliriously, and talking wildly." A doctor visited but seemingly suspected nothing. On another occasion, Marie offered Madame Eichenberg's children some sweets. All of the children who ate them were sick, but it did not cross anyone's mind that Marie Jeanneret was a poisoner.

After leaving the nursing school in Lausanne, Marie moved to Geneva. A new private convalescent hospital (maison de santé) had opened, and Marie successfully applied for a job as a nurse. The owner of the establishment, Madame Juvet, took to Marie.

Shortly after taking the position at the hospital, Madame Juvet's daughter, Julie, became sick after accepting and eating a few of Marie's bonbons. The doctor suspected meningitis. Julie died on December 27, 1865.

Shortly after this, Madame Juvet as well as Emile her son became ill. Less than a month after her daughter's death, Madame Juvet joined her in the same grave. Emile survived. Luckily for him, his father had him removed from the hospital and moved elsewhere.

Before Madame Junot and her daughter died, three elderly female patients had also died. Marie had nursed them all. They died in delirium and in excruciating agony. The hospital closed down.

Marie Jeanneret next applied for a position at a hydropathic establishment, eight kilometers outside Geneva. Madame Vidart, the widow of the owner and doctor of the hydro-establishment, interviewed Marie. After the interview had concluded, Madame Vidart wrote a letter to a doctor in Geneva, requesting from him information about Marie Jeanneret's qualifications and character.

"Don't employ her," was the reply. "All of her patients have a habit of dying."

Needless to say, Marie Jeanneret was not offered a job. Marie did secure a job nursing Madame Lenoir, an elderly lady suffering from inflammation of the lungs. In Marie's care, she also died.

Various other jobs followed. The pattern was the same. Whatever establishment or household Marie entered, people would become violently sick or die.

Marie, while living at the Pension Desarzens, became friends with a Mademoiselle Fritzges. Marie made her new friend a glass of lemonade and shortly after drinking it Mademoiselle Fritzges became ill and delirious.

A doctor was called by the owners of the pension. The doctor immediately recognized the symptoms of belladonna poisoning and suspected foul play. Mademoiselle Fritzges was immediately removed to the local hospital. The doctor on duty at the hospital, a Doctor Rapin, came to the same conclusion. In talking to the doctor who had admitted Mademoiselle Fritzges, Marie Jeanneret's name arose. Doctor Rapin had heard rumors about Marie Jeanneret. She had earned a reputation that whatever home she entered as either a nurse or guest a death would always occur.

## MARIE JEANNERET

"She Mixed Up a Tempting Effervescent Beverage and Handed It to Berthe Who Drank it Eagerly."

Doctor Rapin compiled a dossier of what he knew of Marie Jeanneret and went to visit the police and told them of his suspicions.

The symptoms of Belladonna poisoning are excessive dryness of the mouth, burning and constriction of the throat, dilatation of the pupils, nausea, and occasionally vomiting. There is also excitement of the central nervous system, with hallucinations leading to delirium, giddiness, a staggering gait, rapid pulse, flushed face, drowsiness, and difficulty breathing.

Marie Jeanneret was arrested and a long inquiry followed. The corpses of many, but not all, of the suspected victims were exhumed. Many were not exhumed because they lay outside the jurisdiction of Geneva and in other cases relatives of victims she might have killed did not suspect that a murder had taken place.

When she eventually came to court, the charge against her was that between 1807 and 1818 she had murdered six people and attempted murdering two others. Before Marie's trial started, the Judge ordered her to be examined by three mental health experts. After many hours of examination, the experts concluded:

> *"that there was discernible in her no sign of feeble-mindedness or feeble alienation".*

Marie Jeanneret's jury found her guilty of murdering six people and the attempted murder of two others by the administration of poisonous drugs.

The Jury, however, found themselves unable to condemn a woman to death and added that the crime had "extenuating circumstances." This meant the court was unable to sentence Marie to anything in excess of twenty years. If Marie Jeanneret had been born a man, she would most likely have had her head chopped off at the neck.

Following this verdict, it was felt that it would be unreasonable to punish other murderers in a more severe manner than Marie Jeanneret. Shortly after Marie's trial, capital punishment was abolished in Geneva.

Marie Jeanneret died in 1884 in the prison of St. Antonio, Geneva.

*Prison of St. Antonio, Geneva.*

# MARIA CATHERINA SWANENBURG

Maria Catherina Swanenburg was born on the 9th **of** September in 1839 in Leiden, Netherlands. On the 13th of May in 1868, she married Johannes van der Linden. Together, they had five sons and two daughters. Maria was affectionately known in Leiden as "Goeie Mie," meaning "Good Me," for nursing ill people and children in her home town.

In 1883, she was found poisoning the Groothuizen family. This opened up an investigation into other deaths of people in her care. The investigation looked into one hundred suspicious deaths including her parents' deaths in 1880. It is believed that her mother Johanna was her first victim followed shortly after by her father, both of whom she had taken out insurance on. Her preferred method of poisoning was arsenic.

It was estimated that she poisoned close to eighty people. Twenty-seven died in the years 1880-1883. Another fifty people she had tried to kill survived but as a result of the poisoning, suffered lifelong chronic health problems. Maria's motive was money. She would insure their lives before beginning to poison them.

Her trial started on April 23rd, 1885. Maria was found guilty and sentenced to life in prison. Maria Swanenburg died in prison in 1915.

# JANE TOPPAN

Jane Toppan was born in 1857 and named Honora Kelley. She was the second eldest daughter of Irish immigrants. Her sister, Delia Josephine, was two years older than her. When she was a small child Bridget Kelley, her mother, died from tuberculosis. Her father, known as "Kelly the Crack," was Peter Kelley, an eccentric and an alcoholic. There is a story that when he was a tailor, he sewed his eyelids closed. Whether this is true or not is unknown, but it demonstrates how people perceived his eccentricity or possibly insanity.

Peter Kelley, shortly after his wife died, took Delia and Honora to a Boston orphanage and never saw them again. Reports from the orphanage state that the young girls were, "saved from an extremely miserable home."." In 1864, at the age of just seven, Honora was sent to live in Lowell, Massachusetts in the home of Ann Toppan as a servant. Honora, although never officially adopted by the Toppan family, took their surname and changed her Christian name to Jane. She spent her years with the family in the shadow of Elizabeth, her privileged and pretty foster sister. Jane claimed in later years that Ann Toppan abused her.

Jane's sister, Delia, remained at the orphanage until 1868. Delia was eventually found a place in New York, at the age of twelve, as a servant. When old enough, she left domestic service and became a prostitute and alcoholic. A few years later, Delia was discovered dead in wretched conditions.

Jane, in 1885, enrolled to become a trainee nurse at the Cambridge Hospital. It was during her training that Jane started experimenting with her patients. Her experiments involved altering the patients' prescribed dosages of atropine and morphine. Jane would spend much time on her own with her "special" patients and would make up false charts and medicate them so they would drift in and out of consciousness before dying. On occasions, she would go so far as to climb into their beds with them. No one knows whether she participated in sexual activities with these patients.

Jane earned considerable respect during her time at Cambridge as a ward sister. She was known as a "jolly" nurse and seen as a good sport. In 1889, Jane Toppan was endorsed for a placement at the Massachusetts General, a hospital with a prestigious reputation. Here, she carried on her activities but was dismissed within a year. Jane returned to her previous job at Cambridge Hospital but within months was fired for irresponsibly prescribing opiates.

Jane then began private nursing and seemed to be successful, despite grumbles of minor stealing.

In 1895, she murdered her landlords and in 1899, Jane gave Elizabeth Toppan, her foster sister, a fatal amount of strychnine. At some point in 1901, she was employed to nurse an elderly widower, Alden Davis, who lived in Cataumet. She lived in the house with the family. Alden Davis's wife had been, unknown to the family, killed by Jane.

Within weeks of moving into the house, Alden Davis and both his daughters had died.

Jane returned to Boston where she started to make moves on Elizabeth's, her foster sister's, husband. She poisoned her sister who died and poisoned him slightly, so she would be able to nurse him and return him to good health. In her mind, he would then realize what a terrific nurse she was. Her plot didn't work, and she was thrown out of the house.

Meanwhile in Cataumet, the relatives of Alden Davis requested a toxicology report on the daughters of Alden Davis. This toxicology examination concluded that they had died from poisoning. On October 26th, 1901, Jane Toppan was placed under arrest for murder.

Under interrogation, Jane confessed to thirty-one murders. She claimed that she climbed into bed with her patients as she experienced a sexual thrill from being near someone so close to death. Jane said of her behavior that she wanted:

# JANE TOPPAN

## *"to have killed more people-helpless people-than any other man or woman who ever lived,"*

On June 23rd, 1902 in the County Court at Barnstable, Jane was found to be not guilty as she was insane and was committed to spending the rest of her days in the Insane Asylum in Taunton.

In newspaper reports she was called the "Angel of Death." The *New York Journal* claimed that she had confessed to her lawyer:

## *"that she wanted the jury to find her insane so she could*

## *eventually have a chance at being released,"*

Jane spent her last years frightened of being poisoned by the hospital guards and threatened them with "revenge." She remained at Taunton until her death of natural causes in 1938, when she was eighty-four-years-old.

# AMY ARCHER-GILLIGAN

Amy Duggan Archer-Gilligan, née Duggan, was born in October 1868 in Litchfield, Connecticut. Amy was the eighth child born to James Duggan and Mary Kennedy.

In 1897, Amy married James Archer and in December of 1897, they had a daughter Mary. In 1904, the Archers opened a boarding house, "Sister Amy's Nursing Home for the Elderly", in Newington, Connecticut. They soon built up a reputation as genteel caregivers for the area's wealthy elderly providing nurturing tonics and nutritional meals, despite neither Amy nor James having any medical qualifications. It was an era when there were no regulations governing nursing homes.

The home was so successful that, within six years, they upgraded to a larger property in nearby Windsor. Shortly after the move in 1910, James Archer died. His death certificate issued by the local coroner, Dr. King, said the cause of death was kidney disease. A few weeks before James's death, Amy had insured his life, and the day after James funeral, at which she cried profusely and was comforted by Dr. King, she visited the insurance office.

## NURSES WHO MURDER

Amy's care home rates were considered exceptionally reasonable. She would charge $7 per week or a one-time upfront fee of $1,500 for lifetime care. However for Amy's home, with only fourteen paid beds, to remain profitable, she realized that she needed a constant supply of fresh patients.

Between 1907 and 1910, twelve of Amy's patients had died. Given the ages of the patients, four deaths per year were not considered suspicious. However, after James's death, that number began to rise significantly.

The increase in deaths in the summer of 1911 was partly attributed to the unprecedented heat wave that hit the northeastern United States. More than 3,000 deaths had been attributed to this natural disaster. Yet even after the heat wave had finished, the elderly patients in Amy's home continued to die. Dr. King attributed each death to old age.

In 1913, Amy met and married a rich widower, Michael Gilligan. Soon after the wedding, he changed his will leaving his entire estate to Amy. On the 20$^{th}$ of February in 1914, Michael died after eating one of Amy's special nutritional dinners. Dr. King gave the cause of death as "natural causes".

Many of Amy's patients had no relatives to keep an eye out for them, but one resident, Franklin Andrews, an apparently healthy man, had a sister, Nellie Pierce, who regularly visited him. When he died unexpectedly on May 29, 1914, Nellie became suspicious. The

## AMY ARCHER-GILLIGAN

cause of her brother's death, according to Dr. King was a gastric ulcer. Going through her brother's papers, Nellie noted that Franklin had just signed an agreement allowing Amy to withdraw a large amount of money. Nellie began watching the obituary column in the local paper and began to feel evermore alarmed by the number of deaths occurring at the home.

Nellie, as her suspicions grew, went to the district attorney's office and reported her findings. The District Attorney checked the death certificates and seemed satisfied that everything was in order.

Nellie then went to see a journalist at the *Hartford Courant* and relayed her suspicions to him. He promised to investigate.

The reporter discovered that there had been forty-eight deaths at the home over a five-year period and that shortly before each death, the elderly patient had signed over to Amy large sums of money. Dr. Howard King had signed the death certificates in each case as due to natural causes. The journalist, by consulting with other physicians around Connecticut, learned that an average death toll in a small establishment as Amy's would be eight to ten over a five-year period, not forty-eight.

The reporter wrote up his story on May 9, 1916, and entitled it "The Murder Factory".

The story forced the police to investigate. Armed with a search warrant, they raided "Sister Amy's Nursing Home for the Elderly". In the clinic's storerooms, the police found large amounts

## NURSES WHO MURDER

of bottled arsenic. Amy explained that they were to keep the rats under control. The police did not believe her and requested the local judge for permission to exhume some of the patient's bodies as well as that of Amy's last husband, Michael Gilligan. Altogether, five bodies were exhumed, and all were found to have died either by arsenic or strychnine poisoning.

Amy was arrested and charged with five counts of murder. Her trial took place in Hartford, Connecticut in June of 1917. Amy pleaded not guilty. On June 18, 1917, a jury found her guilty. The judge sentenced her to death. Amy appealed and was granted a new trial in 1919 in which she pleaded insanity. Amy's daughter, Mary, testified that her mother was a morphine addict. In this trial, the jury found Amy guilty of second-degree murder, and she was sentenced to life imprisonment.

*Amy Archer-Gilligan*

# AMY ARCHER-GILLIGAN

It soon became obvious to prison authorities by Amy's behavior that she was insane, and she was moved to an insane asylum. She died in 1928, at the age of 59 at the Connecticut state insane asylum.

# BERTHA GIFFORD

Bertha Alice Williams Graham Gifford was born in Grubville, Missouri in 1872. Her parents were early pioneers in eastern Missouri. Bertha's mother, Matilda Caroline Lee, married her father, William Poindexter Williams, on January 1st of 1859, in Jefferson County, Missouri. They had ten children, but two died in early infancy leaving six boys and two girls. The Williams family was known as one of the area's most respectable families. The family was a regular attendee at the local fundamentalist church, the Church of God.

Bertha grew up to be an extraordinarily beautiful woman with dark hair and a dark complexion. As a young woman, she loved to dance and was courted by many. In 1894, when Bertha was twenty-two, she married Henry Graham in Hillsboro, Jefferson County, Missouri. They managed a small boarding house on the edge of Hillsboro town and had a daughter together. The marriage, over time, became an unhappy one, and there were rumors that William was seeing a girl on the sly. When Bertha was thirty and still extremely beautiful, she met Eugene Gifford, a handsome, friendly farmer and carpenter, seven years her junior. When they met, Eugene was betrothed to another girl. Shortly after meeting Eugene, Henry Graham became ill and was diagnosed with pneumonia. Bertha nursed him conscientiously, never leaving his bedside. Although Henry was physically strong, he developed what doctors called complications, and he died at the age of 34 suffering from violent, excruciating, stomach cramps.

In 1907, after waiting a respectable amount of time and allowing Eugene to break off his engagement and Bertha to collect her insurance payout on Henry's death, Bertha and Eugene married. Once married, Bertha and Eugene moved away from Jefferson County to Catawissa, Franklin County, Missouri. Catawissa was an extremely small rural community 39 miles from St. Louis and about 10 miles southwest of the larger and more developed town of Pacific.

Catawissa consisted of not much more than a post office, a church, and a few small stores. Bertha had several relatives by marriage already living in Catawissa. Here, Eugene took up farming, and they lived on a house on Old Bend Road, about one mile from the Meramec River. The people who lived "on the bend" had their own close-knit community separate from the small town of Catawissa. The community was made up of farmers who worked hard and long hours. When Eugene and Bertha moved to the area, the mode of transportation was still by horse and wagon. There were hitching posts and water troughs for horses along the town streets. T. Dermott, a plumber and owner of a stove and tin ware store on

## NURSES WHO MURDER

Catawissa St., purchased the first auto truck for his business in March of 1911. By the end of the 1920's, most businesses bought trucks, but some continued to use horses and wagons into the 1940's.

Eugene soon became popular in the small, close-knit community and gained a reputation as a skilled worker and good company. Bertha gained a reputation as an exceptionally talented cook and in time as a "Good Samaritan" for her help in caring for ill neighbors. She became known and appreciated as a good country nurse and kind neighbor, always ready to lend a helping hand if someone was sick or injured. She was known to ride or walk for miles to help at the site of an accident or attend to the sick. In small, rural communities such as 'the bend' in the early 1900's, it was difficult to get medical help in an emergency. The only doctor in the town of Catawissa, Doctor Hemker, had a large area to cover and was frequently difficult to reach. The newspapers at this time were full of advertisements for lotions and potions for self-medication. Bertha made her own concoctions for treating aches, muscle sprains, coughs, and other ailments.

The people who lived on the bend did their main shopping in the small town of Pacific, which was approximately a forty-five minute journey. Like the other residents of "the bend," Bertha did her main shopping in the town of Pacific. In 1911, Eugene's widowed mother and young brother, Emilie and James Gibbons, moved in with Eugene and Bertha. In 1913, Emilie became ill with stomach cramps and vomiting and died. Bertha took it upon herself to arrange the funeral. A year later in 1914, thirteen-year-old James died in Bertha's arms from similar symptoms to his mother's.

Close neighbors of Bertha's, George and Margaret Stuhlfelder's fifteen-month-old son Bernard became ill with pneumonia in February of 1915. Bertha immediately offered her help to the exhausted, distraught parents. She sat selfishly by his bed, or so her neighbors thought, and when complications to his illness started, she stayed for three long nights and days as the small boy's body writhed around in agony with stomach cramps, before dying in excruciating pain.

One night in 1917, a relative of Eugene's, Sherman Pounds, arrived drunkenly on the doorstep of Bertha's and Eugene's house. Sherman was a large, strong man of fifty-three. He was a widower with five children and on the weekend he liked to drink. Eugene and Bertha helped him in and put him to bed, and Bertha made him a tonic. In the middle of the night, Sherman awoke with terrible stomach cramps and was dead by the morning. The doctor declared the cause of death from drinking.

Eight months later in November, a hired helper of Eugene's, 52-year-old Jim Ogle, who was complaining of being ripped off by the Gibbons, became ill with what Doctor Hemker said was malaria. Bertha kindly offered to take charge of all nursing duties. On November 17th, Bertha visited Pacific to stock up on a few items. While there, she called into the pharmacy and complained to the pharmacist, known as "Uncle Jimmy," that rats were attacking her chickens. He suggested an arsenic based rat poison for which she signed for in the poison register. The following day, Jim became sicker and complained of severe stomach cramps. The doctor was sent for and, after examining Jim, said the stomach pains were a result of the malaria. For three days, Jim suffered agonizing pain before dying on November 20$^{th}$. Dr. Hemker wrote, "Gastritis" on the certificate as having caused the death.

Five years later in December of 1922, Sherman's three-year-old granddaughter, Beulah Pounds, was left in Bertha's care for the afternoon while her mother went Christmas shopping in Pacific. When Beulah's mother returned to pick her up, her daughter complained of stomach pains. Bertha and the mother decided it would be best to leave Beulah overnight with Bertha. The following morning, Beulah was much sicker and in an enormous amount of pain. Her mother sent for the doctor, but Beulah was dead before he arrived. Bertha described Beulah's symptoms to him, and Dr. Hemker wrote out a death certificate listing the cause of death as gastritis. Beulah was buried on January 5, 1923. It was one local funeral Bertha failed to attend, and Bertha loved funerals. Bertha was fuming because Beulah's Aunt had suggested a post-mortem should be done on Beulah. The aunt was unhappy, as her father Sherman had similarly died in Bertha's house from severe stomach pains. However, because the doctor didn't think anything was amiss and the parents thinking it would cost too much money, failed to perform an autopsy.

Six years almost to the day that George and Margaret Stuhlfelder's son Bernard had died, Margaret, their two-year-old daughter, became ill with pneumonia. They sent for Dr. Hemker who prescribed medication for her. Then Bertha arrived to help. She was dressed in a white apron and carried her bag of tonics. She told Margaret that she thought the baby looked terribly ill and did not think she would recover. Nevertheless, Bertha sat by the baby's bed. Two days later Margaret started vomiting, and three days later Margaret died in agony.

In March of 1923, George and Margaret's daughter Irene, seven-years-old, became ill with stomach pains. Once again, the Stuhlfelder's called the doctor who prescribed stomach medication. This appeared to ease her pain and then Bertha called by to help nurse her. Shortly after Bertha's arrival, Irene began to vomit and a few days later, she died in agony. The doctor filled out the death certificate clearly thinking there was nothing amiss.

Another local family, George and Ethel Schamel, were also friends of the Giffords. George frequently helped Elmer out on the farm. The family had intended to leave Catawissa and move to St Louis in April of 1923 but after only three weeks in St Louis, they returned to Catawissa. Two years later in June of 1925, Ethel at the age of 33, became ill, and Bertha nursed her, but Ethel died. Eight weeks later Lloyd, George and Ethel's son, who was just nine-years-old, died of gastritis while sleeping over at Bertha's house. This death was followed eight weeks later by the brother Elmer's death, at the age of seven, also from gastritis who Bertha had also helped nurse. Barely a month later, George Schamel's sister, Leona, became ill and started vomiting. Bertha nursed her. Leona died in October at the age of thirty-seven. Doctor Hemker had signed all of the deaths certificated as gastroenteritis.

It was after the Schamel boys' deaths, Lloyd and Elmer that people began to talk. The deaths had happened almost one after the other in such a short time, and both the Schamel boys had been so healthy and full of life.

Maybe people had thought Bertha's presence at so many deathbeds was odd before but had never voiced it. Now, it began to be discussed openly, as was the fact that Bertha enjoyed reading about murders and accidents in the newspapers and enjoyed talking about them.

All of this was going on against the backdrop of prohibition. Many of the country folk had stills in their barns and were wary of the authorities and attracting attention. Eugene Gifford had a large whisky still in one of his barns and a friend of his, Gus, would sell the whisky in the nearby towns of Pacific, Catawissa, and neighboring areas. Eugene and Gus had some kind of squabble over the proceeds, and Bertha was so mad at Gus she chased him with a butcher's knife.

# BERTHA GIFFORD

*LLYOD's DEATH CERTIFICATE*

A short while later in 1926, Gus's mother became ill and Bertha, forgetting the fight, offered to nurse her. Gus's mother died.

One evening on May 15th, 1927, Edward Brinley, an alcoholic, ex-butcher from Pacific, who was now working for Eugene as a farmhand, collapsed in a drunken stupor in front of Bertha's front door. Eugene found him and helped Edward into bed. In the morning, Bertha gave him some of her homemade lemonade.

# NURSES WHO MURDER

A few hours later, he developed chronic stomach pains and died in agony in the afternoon. Doctor Hemker, feeling nervous with all the gossip about Bertha in the vicinity, decided to consult with another doctor from Pacific as to the cause of death. It would seem they could not agree as two different diagnoses were written on the death certificate.

> *"acute unknown disease and acute gastritus, cause unknown."*

## BERTHA GIFFORD

No post-mortem was called for. Bertha called the undertaker and organized the funeral.

This latest death caused all the talk about Bertha to start up again, only this time it became much more widespread and reached the ears of Frank Jenny, a young up-and-coming prosecuting attorney. Six months following the death of Edward, a grand jury of Franklin County began investigations into the rumors and deaths surrounding Bertha.

Bertha Gifford was furious. How dare they think such things about her when all she had done was tried to help people? Bertha threatened to sue for libel anyone who uttered a bad word against her. Eugene was also enraged that people should say such things against his Bertha and, normally placid, he would hurl abuse at anyone he suspected of gossiping about Bertha being a killer. If it was a strategy, it worked. People, who had been scheduled to give evidence in front of the Grand Jury, lost their tongues. The Grand Jury was unwilling to indict Bertha as they felt there was insufficient evidence.

This led to many believing that the Gifford's had friends in high places that had put a stop to the investigation. However, Frank Jenny, the young, ambitious prosecutor, was a Rottweiler and was not going to give up. Just months later, he was equipped with the record books of poisons bought from two pharmacists in Pacific that showed Bertha had been buying abnormal amounts of arsenic since 1911, "For rats," she had written next to her numerous signatures, and with witnesses that were now eager to talk, he tried again.

When the second investigation began, Bertha and Eugene left Catawissa and moved to Eureka, Missouri. The story before long became plastered across newspapers all over the US. As the news circulated, Frank Jenny's office began to receive phone calls and letters from people claiming their relatives or friends had passed away while being attended by Bertha. Soon the official number of questionable deaths climbed from nine up to seventeen.

On August 23, 1928, the jury returned an indictment charging Bertha Gifford with two counts of first-degree murder in the deaths of Edward Brinley and Elmer Schamel.

On August 25$^{th}$, 1928, Police Detective Andrew McDonnell arrested Bertha in Eureka. Chief McDonnell drove Bertha to the station in Union and gently questioned her. Over a cup of tea, they talked about a range of things. Bertha began talking about all the gossip about her and the story that she had killed the little girl Beulah with arsenic. She thoroughly denied giving arsenic to Beulah but said she had given it to Elmer and Lloyd Schamel and also Edward Brinley, just to help ease their pain. Later on in the conversation, she admitted to Andrew McDonnell that she may have given arsenic to one or two others. Chief Andrew McDonnell wrote out her confession. Bertha was then driven to jail in Union.

## BERTHA GIFFORD

The following day the newspapers printed her confession, and Bertha was mortified. She hysterically denied the confession and said the statement was a pack of lies. Eugene gave statements to the reporters saying that his wife was frightened and agitated, and that is why she had confessed.

Eugene hired a top lawyer, James Booth, who pleaded not guilty to the court on Bertha Gifford's behalf.

In September of 1928, the corpses of Edward Brinley and Elmer and Lloyd Schamel were exhumed. In their bodies, significant amounts of arsenic were found.

The health commissioner of the state made a statement criticizing the doctor in Catawissa. In the statement, he declared that:

*"It is a physician's duty to determine the cause of death before filing a death certificate," and ordered the Bureauof VitalStatistics to refuse to accept any certificate lacking a "concise and clear statement of the cause of death."*

Bertha's trial began in the courthouse of Union on November 19th of 1928. It was a prominent newspaper story and made

## NURSES WHO MURDER

headlines around the country. A murder trial was a significant event: something to look forward to, and something worth gossip and speculation.

*NEWSPAPERS HAD A FIELD DAY*

Reporters and crowds of people filled the courtroom and corridors, and those who could not fit in the courtroom lined the steps outside waiting to hear details. Bertha's name was on everyone's lips. Surprise was registered as a story of her beauty in her younger days was revealed, for the Bertha that appeared in the courtroom on that cold November day was anything but beautiful. The newspapers described Bertha as thick and heavyset, with a weather-beaten, furrowed face and eyes that were dead.

Rumors as to her behavior in jail wove through the crowd like Chinese whispers. There were tales of Bertha hiding under a blanket in her jail cell in the day and at night, wearing a blood red robe as she paced up and down howling like a werewolf or clutching the bars at the window and hurling curses out the window. The whispers continued with tales of how Bertha would only eat ice cream and that she refused to talk to anyone except Eugene and would do so only if dressed in a pristine white nurse's uniform.

During the four-day trial, both the prosecution and defense agreed on one thing: that Bertha Gifford was insane. The prosecution argued for her to be locked up for life, while the defense wanted the possibility of release if she recovered.

The jury took just three hours to reach their decision that Bertha Gifford had murdered Edward Brinley and the Schamel brothers while insane and remained insane. The judge sentenced her to a life of confinement in the mentally insane unit of the State Hospital in Farmington, Missouri.

Although Bertha was only tried and convicted for three murders, the true number during 1909-1927 is believed to be at least seventeen.

Bertha Gifford died on August 20, 1951. She had spent close to twenty-three years in Farmington. After her death, Eugene had her body taken to Pacific for a private funeral at the cemetery in Morse

Mill. The grave is unmarked.

The trial, in the end, revealed very little; just a great many unanswered questions. How had Bertha walked free among her neighbors for so many years and killed so many? Why, after so many deaths, had the doctor just signed every certificate without a post-mortem with the same woman present at every death? What about Eugene? What did he know?

Eugene remained living in Eureka. He died in 1957 and any answers to any questions he took with him.

# Marie Fikáková

Marie Fikáčková was born to poor German parents on September 9th, 1936 in Sušice, a beautiful, historic city in Czechoslovakia.

In 1945 when World War II ended, many Germans living in Czechoslovakia suffered from Czech hostilities towards them. Marie's family was one of them. Her father was a violent alcoholic who hated the Czechs with a passion. Neither was she close to her mother with whom she often quarreled. Her one brother was mentally handicapped. Despite Marie's dysfunctional home life, she did well at school. In 1955, she successfully passed the Secondary Medical Service School examinations in Klatovy. She then found work as a nurse at the Sušice National Health Centre. In 1957, Marie was transferred to the Obstetrics department. Marie was liked and respected by her colleagues for being amiable and industrious and within a short amount of time was being considered for promotion to Head Nurse. There was, however, one insurmountable problem for Marie: much as she enjoyed her work in the maternity ward, she had an almost complete intolerance to the crying of new born babies.

## NURSES WHO MURDER

Many women take to babies easily, knowing how to hold the baby in a relaxed manner that soothes the fretful newborn. Marie was not such a woman.

On February 23rd, 1960, two newborn baby girls died on the maternity ward of the Sušice National Health Centre. During the autopsies of the babies, it was found that both infants had numerous broken bones in their arms along with head trauma, which had caused their deaths.

The authorities began to interview all of the staff involved in the care and delivery of the babies. On February 28th, 1960, twenty-four-year-old Marie was interviewed. The interview turned into a six hour interrogation as the authorities became uneasy at Marie's answers to various questions.

During the interview, she claimed that as a child she was tortured by her mentally ill brother and abused by her father. At midnight, after six hours of questioning, Marie finally admitted to killing the baby girls.

She said:

*"When I was pressing little Prosserova's head, I could feel my fingers sinking into it. I did not feel any skull cracking at that time. I was just pressing the little head and my fingers got deeper and deeper. My anger faded away after a while and I could continue working."*

To Marie, it was a solution to child quieting: when using 'pressure point therapy' the baby never cried again. In explanation, she claimed that the crying babies affected her concentration, she hated crying babies, they put her off her work, and she was intent on getting a promotion. She said she would even hit her own child if it cried very often. Luckily, she didn't have one. She claimed that she only felt this way when she was menstruating. Marie confessed in the interrogation to having murdered ten newborn babies since 1957. The hospital and the authorities kept quiet about Marie's confessions to the other killings.

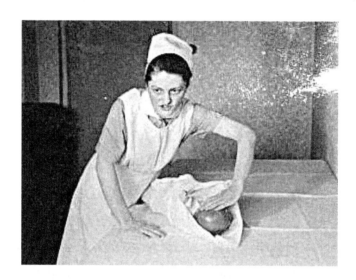

At her trial, she was charged with only two murders as there was no evidence to the other killings she had claimed to have committed. At her trial, a number of people testified to her explosive personality. Neighbor's testified that she terrorized her mentally handicapped brother regularly and that she possessed a violent streak.

On October 6th, 1960, Marie Fikáčková was sentenced to death by hanging. Her lawyer appealed the sentence twice but on each occasion, the appeals were denied.

The execution took place early in the morning of April 13th, 1961 in Pankrác prison.

Marie Fikáčková's trial and execution were kept secret in communist-occupied Czechoslovakia, the government not wishing its citizens or foreigners to know that under their regime such crimes occurred.

Following the collapse of the communist government in 1996, many secret files were uncovered, one of which was Marie Fikáčková's. TV Nova, the Czech commercial television station, broadcast the story on January 4th, 2007.

# CECILE BOMBEEK a.k.a. Sister Godfrida.

Cecile Bombeek was born in 1933 in the East Flanders province of Belgium, to strict catholic parents. As a young woman she became a nun of the Apostolic Congregation of St. Joseph and became known as Sister Godfrida. She trained to become a nurse.

In time, she became the geriatrics manager of a thirty-eight bed ward in a public hospital in the quiet, picturesque marketing town of Wetteren. Sister Godfrida shared an expensive fancy apartment near to the hospital with another nun who taught in a local school. It was later discovered that they were lovers. It was also discovered that she was simultaneously having a sexual relationship with a retired priest. In her apartment, they enjoyed expensive food and vintage wine and would often dine out together in Wetteren's best restaurants.

Sometime during the 1970s, Sister Godfrida underwent brain surgery. Following the surgery, she became a morphine addict. In 1976, the other nuns working on the geriatric ward began to notice that a large number of their patients were dying. Twenty-one patients had died in a year. They began to keep a diary that recorded not only the deaths and the surrounding circumstances of each one but also a

## CECILE BOMBEEK a.k.a. Sister Godfrida.

variety of incidents that appeared to be the sadistic maltreatment of old people, such as catheters ripped out from the bladders of the patients by "persons unknown".

Meanwhile, several elderly patients complained of being robbed of their money. An internal investigation showed Sister Godfrida to be the culprit. She had stolen over $30,000 from her patients to support her morphine habit.

In August of 1977, Sister Godfrida was suspended from the hospital and was sent to a private clinic for drug addiction treatment in Ghent. She returned to the hospital in January of 1978 and appeared unchanged. It is thought that her flat mate and lover, who visited her in the drug addiction hospital, had kept her supplied with morphine.

With her behavior unchanged, the other nurses took their diaries and suspicions to the hospital administrator. Dr. De Corte was ordered to carry out an investigation. Meanwhile, the police had been waiting to question Sister Godfrida about the thefts of money. They took her in for questioning, where she admitted to having killed three patients between seventy-five and eighty-years-old with overdoses of insulin. When asked why, she replied, "Because they were too noisy at night." She insisted that she had done it "nicely," and none of them had suffered.

The Belgium police formally charged Sister Godfrida, at the age of forty four, with three murders and the theft of $30,000. She was detained in jail in the nearby town of Ghent. The judge in Ghent ordered exhumations of the bodies of the three patients that the nun had admitted killing but also those of other possible victims.

When the story hit the newspapers the townspeople of Wetteren were reeling from shock that the short, plump, cherub-faced nun, Sister Godfrida, was a serial killer.

Although only officially charged with killing three patients, the suspected number is believed to be more than thirty.

*Court House Ghent*

In March of 1978, the Judge committed Sister Godfrida for psychiatric observation.

Sister Godfrida was found to be mentally insane and unfit for trial and interred in a psychiatric facility.

# " LAINZ ANGELS OF DEATH"

As if it's not shocking and horrifying enough that one nurse goes on a killing spree in Vienna, Austria, four nurses collaborated together in the murder of their patients. The killing spree was begun by Waltraud Wagner who was born in 1960. Waltraud worked in the geriatric ward, "pavilion five," of Lainz General Hospital. Waltraud had become a nurse because she wanted to help people. Working on the geriatric ward she liked to make her patients comfortable and help ease their suffering and pain.

All of the patients on her ward were elderly, and many of them had terminal illnesses. In 1983, an elderly seventy-seven-year-old female patient begged Waltraud to "end her pain and suffering." The woman repeated her impassioned appeal several times daily to the twenty-three-year-old Waltraud. The nurse reflected over the appeals when she was off duty and decided that if her death was inevitable, perhaps it was more humane to end her suffering. The next time the woman begged her to end her suffering, Nurse Waltraud walked determinedly to the medicine store and took out a lethal dose of morphine. As she injected it into the IV tube, she was convinced that she had done the right thing as the look of pain and anguish on the patient's face changed to one of serenity.

That day, Waltraud finished her work at the hospital feeling energized. She also discovered that she rather enjoyed having power over life and death, and the ability to relieve someone of so much pain. When more patients begged her to end their pain and suffering, she obliged.

After work, Waltraud would frequently go for drinks in a bar near the hospital with three nurses who worked on her ward: Maria Gruber, who was nineteen, Ilene Leidolf, who was twenty-one, and Stephanija Mayer, a native Yugoslavian who was forty-three. Inevitably, they would discuss their days' work. Waltraud, suggested to them that she thought patients who asked should be put out of their misery. The other nurses agreed, saying how much it upset them to see the patients suffering so badly.

The following day, Waltraud taught the nurses how to administer the right amount of morphine for a mercy killing. They saw it as an act of grace and felt no guilt. At first, the nurses killed only occasionally and only the most seriously ill patients, but by 1987, the deaths began to escalate. Now all four nurses were enjoying their new found sense of power.

The nurses began to meet nightly in the bar and over drinks decide who their next patient to be terminated would be. They would joke about who was to get the next "ticket to God." Their killing had moved from compassion to sadism. To prevent questions about the amounts of morphine being used on the ward, they also used Rohypnol and Insulin. Within the hospital, rumors began to spread that there was a murderer on "Pavilion Five." Consequently, Waltraud invented a new way of terminating the patients which she named the "water therapy". Many elderly patients suffer from fluid on the lungs and so her new barbaric treatment could not be detected if an autopsy was performed.

The "water therapy" consisted of one of the nurses holding the selected victim down and holding their nose while Waltraud poured a jug of water down the patient's throat. This would cause the lungs to fill with water, and the patient would drown in their bed. This was an excruciating, torturous, painful death for the patient but would be undiscoverable as murder.

The nurses no longer made any pretence among themselves about mercy killings. They now handed out their "Tickets to God" for patients that had soiled their bed or just simply annoyed them. The four nurses distributed their tickets unhindered from 1983 to 1989.

**AFTER WORK**

One evening in early 1989, the four nurses met in the bar as normal and discussed their day's work. This particular evening as they consumed more drinks, their voices and laughter got louder. A doctor at a nearby table sat in shock as he listened to the four nurses joking and laughing in minute detail about that day's "ticket winner" who had suffered enormous distress but, in their opinion, had well earned her fate.

The doctor left the bar greatly distressed and went immediately to inform the police before alerting the hospital administrators. An investigation was immediately launched.

The head doctor of "Pavilion Five" and the four nurses were suspended. A number of the patients' bodies who had died on the ward were exhumed for pathological tests. Most of them had water in the lungs, but others had overdoses of morphine, insulin, or Rohypnol. The investigation lasted six weeks. At the end of it, all four nurses were arrested and charged with murder on the 7th of April, 1989.

The nurses confessed collectively to forty-nine murders during a six year period. Waltraud, at first, accepted responsibility for thirty-nine of the murders but as she spaced the floors of her prison cell awaiting trial she scaled the number down to ten; all, she said, were carried out to put an end to the patient's suffering.

Following a month long trial, they were all found guilty on the 28th of March, 1991. Waltraud Wagner was found guilty of fifteen murders, seventeen attempted murders, and two charges of physical assault. She received a life sentence. Ilene Leidolf was found guilty of five of the murders and received a life sentence. Maria Gruber and Stephanija Mayer were found guilty of attempted murder and manslaughter. They both received fifteen year prison

# "LAINZ ANGELS OF DEATH"

sentences.

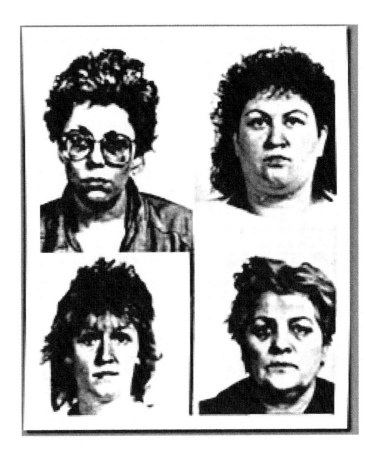

Many people believe that the true numbers murdered were in the hundreds.

The state prosecutor at the end of the trial said:

*"It's a small step from killing the terminally ill to the killing of insolent, burdensome patients, and from there to that which was known under the Third Reich as euthanasia. It is a door that must never be opened again."*

Maria Gruber and Stephanija Mayer were released from prison at the end of the 1990s for good behavior. They were issued with new identities.

Waltraud Wagner and Ilene Leidolf were released from prison on the 7th of August 2008. Prior to their release, they were allowed to leave the prison for day trips to go to the hairdresser or for shopping. The daily outings were part of a prerelease program to help them to adjust to life outside of prison.

Both Waltraud Wagner and Ilene Leidolf were given new identities by the Austrian government.

# GENENE JONES

Genene Anne Jones was born on the 13th of July, 1950 and was immediately handed over for adoption. Dick and Gladys Jones became her new parents. They already had two adopted children, both older than Genene, and later adopted another child, a boy named Travis, who was two years Genene's junior.

They lived just north-west of San Antonio, Texas. A city that is nothing like the stereotypical image of a Texas city. To its credit, it lacks the modern skyline of a large city and neither does it have the tumbleweed-strewn landscape of the Wild West. The Jones lived in a four-bedroom, two-story, house. Rick Jones was a larger than life character, an imposing six feet tall figure, weighing around 240 pounds, and bald. He was a professional gambler and entrepreneur. He also operated nightclubs. When the night clubs went bust, he tried running a restaurant, but that was unsuccessful. His next venture was a billboard company, and he would frequently take one or another of the children in his truck to help him put up the billboards. Later, Genene was to recall that this was one of the happier memories of her life.

As a child, Genene felt slightly left out from the family; she referred to herself as the "black sheep" of the family. She was small and overweight which did not help her insecurities. Sometimes to gain her parents' attention, she would feign illness.

At John Marshall High School, she was known to be bossy and aggressive. Genene worked in the library and if the other students weren't working the way she thought they should be, Genene would tell them what to do.

She also had a reputation for manipulating and lying to people to make her the center of attention. The person she was closest to was her brother Travis. Tragically, at the age of fourteen, he made a pipe bomb. Premature detonation of home made bombs is a danger in constructing any homemade bomb, and it blew up in his face, killing him. At Travis's funeral, Genene, who was only sixteen, howled and fainted. Shortly after this tragedy, her father Dick was found to have terminal cancer. He refused the treatment offered and died in January of 1968, at the age of just fifty-six, just slightly over a year following Travis's tragic accident.

The family was devastated. Genene's mother Gladys began drinking heavily. Following Genene's graduation from High School in 1968, she married James DeLany ("Jimmy"), an overweight high school dropout. The marriage was as if she was attempting to fill an emptiness left by her father and younger brother for her new husband had little interest in anything except hot rods and cars with large engines modified to achieve higher performance and speed.

# GENENE JONES

Seven months following the marriage, Jimmy joined the navy. Left alone, Genene went on a sexual rampage. Her mother, Gladys, who was still supporting Genene, persuaded her to get herself an occupation or a career. Genene eventually listened and enrolled in Mim's Beauty School. Once qualified, she landed a job at a beauty parlor at the Methodist Hospital. Here, she discovered that she enjoyed working in a hospital environment.

When her husband returned home from the navy, Genene became pregnant and gave birth to a son: Richard Michael DeLany born on January 19, 1972. The marriage lasted for four years before Genene left Jimmy. She moved out when he was in the hospital recovering from an accident. She cited violence on her divorce papers for the failure of the marriage.

Not long after the divorce, Genene's oldest brother was diagnosed with cancer and died. Genene began to worry about getting cancer and no longer felt comfortable with handling hair dyes. She decided to begin training to become a nurse, even though she was pregnant with her second child, a daughter she named Heather. Luckily, her mother Gladys was happy to help with the children.

## BEXAR COUNTY HOSPITAL ICU

Genene did well in the one-year nursing program and excelled at her licensed vocational nurse (LVN) examinations on October 18, 1977 and landed her first nursing job at the Methodist

Hospital in San Antonio. Genene appeared competent at her job but resented the fact that in the medical hierarchy she was at the bottom. After only eight months, Genene was discharged for two reasons: there were complaints from a patient concerning rude, inappropriate behavior and also her attempts at making judgments where she lacked the necessary authority. Her next job did not last too long either at the obstetrics-gynecology ward at Community Hospital. Genene then found work at Bexar County Medical Center Hospital in the ICU pediatric unit. She was never asked for what reasons she was dismissed from her last jobs. It was at the Bexar County that she left a tragic and horrifying mark.

Genene began working in the pediatric intensive care unit on October 30, 1978. The head nurse in the unit, Pat Belko, liked Genene and saw her as an enthusiastic, hard-working, dedicated nurse with knowledge and technical skill above that of most LVNs. Genene, knowing that Pat Belko held her in such high regard, made her feel special and superior to the other nurses on the unit. The other nurses disliked her. They found her foul-mouthed and disliked her graphic details of her sexual conquests. Genene would bully new nurses on the ward and would insist they report to her. More than one nurse transferred out of the unit to escape her bullying and tyrannical personality.

Genene would also, on occasion, refuse orders from nurses senior to her saying, "She would do what was best for the child." The other nurses soon recognized that Genene enjoyed feeling needed and particularly liked attending to the very ill on her three to eleven p.m. shift. The doctor in charge of the unit, James Robotham like Pat Belko, liked Genene. He, too, saw her as a hard-working dedicated nurse. He was impressed by her many questions and how eager she was to learn. Genene had the nickname "Robotham's pet," bestowed on her by the other nurses.

Genene's most distinguishing medical skill was her ability at inserting intravenous lines (IVs) into veins. Many patients are put on IVs to provide direct access to a vein. This could be used for injecting drugs, drawing blood, or giving fluids. For many nurses, inserting IVs is a daily chore, but one that many never master as veins move under the skin, making it easy to miss a few times before hitting the right spot. With a baby, it is even more difficult as their veins are only the size of a thread. Genene, however, never found any vein too small or any patient too restless. One doctor said of her, "She could stick an IV in a freaking fly."

The intensive care pediatric unit where Genene worked was a rectangular room about 26 feet long by 24 feet wide. It contained eight beds, in separate cubicles, with large glass windows that allowed the nurses to keep an eye on the patients and on the machines that monitored their heartbeats and breathing. At the back of the unit was a small sitting area for the nurses to sit and relax. A large cupboard contained equipment and supplies for conducting simple lab tests.

## NURSES WHO MURDER

The patients' ages treated in the ICU ranged from a few months up to sixteen-years-old. Newborn babies were kept in a separate neonatal ICU on a lower floor of the hospital. Children were brought to the ICU after surgery or to be treated for an injury or a disease.

A pediatric nurse in the ICU unit normally has one or two patients assigned to her who demand almost constant attention. For the first three months at the hospital, Genene worked nights before moving to the 3 p.m. to 11 p.m. shift. Bexar County hospital had a nursing shortage, and Genene would often volunteer to work overtime.

Genene thrived on the excitement of an emergency, and even if it was not one of her patient's, she would involve herself in the situation. If a child died, Genene would cry and then offer to carry the body to the morgue. A chore most other nurses detested.

In the pediatric intensive care unit where Genene worked, a medical emergency was known as a code. A code would begin if a nurse noticed, for example, that a child had difficulty breathing or his or her heart beat had become irregular or had stopped. In these situations, the nurse would alert the nursing station, who would then press a white emergency button. This would bring doctors running to the pediatric ICU. If a nurse believed there was a severe emergency, she would alert the nursing station to a "code blue". In this case, a switchboard operator would send a message over the public address system announcing, "Code blue to Pedi ICU", which would summon help throughout the hospital. ICU nurses would then race to the patient with a "crash cart," loaded with equipment and emergency drugs. Doctors, medical students, respiratory therapists, pharmacists, and others would rush to the ICU. In the center of all this activity would be the patient's nurse, who put in the code. These were the situations that Genene thrived on, as she would be very much the center of attention being the nurse in charge of the patient.

At Bexar County Hospital ICU if a child died, the child's nurse was responsible for delivering the body to the morgue in the basement. Frequently, the child's parents would wish to hold the child before it was taken to the morgue. The nurse would first have to wash off the blood from the body and remove any catheters or tubes. When the parents had finished their "goodbyes," the nurse would then call the security guard and deliver the body to the morgue.

In 1980, less than a year after gaining her RN degree, twenty-five-year-old Suzanna Maldonado began work in the pediatric ICU. She worked the eleven-to-seven shift; the shift following Genene's. Suzanna took a dislike to Genene, finding her aggressive, rude, and arrogant.

When shifts changed every eight hours, the nurses going off duty would meet for a "report," with the nurses coming on duty. At this meeting, the nurses would describe the state of their patients and any special problems for which to be on the lookout. Suzanna disliked Genene's predictions of gloom and doom and her harrowing predictions of which child was going to die. She also noticed how she scared the new nurses.

To the parents of the critically ill patients, Genene showed an entirely different personality. She would patiently listen to their complaints and fears and have long chats with them. She would become their friend and call them by their first names.

More and more of these "code blue" emergencies began to occur on the 3 p.m. to 11 p.m. shift, with many of the babies dying. Suzanna Maldonado was among the first to notice that they all coincidentally happened on Genene's shift and were normally her patients. Suzanne began taking notes and watching Genene carefully. Other nurses and doctors began talking about the number of children dying in the pediatric ICU from problems that were not normally fatal.

"They're going to start thinking I'm the Death Nurse," Genene joked to other nurses one day. After a two week period in the unit when seven children had died during the 3 p.m. to 11 p.m. shift, the shift became known around the hospital as the death shift. The rumors and gossip about Genene began to intensify. Her boss Pat Belko defended her, believing it was just malicious gossip from the other nurses who were jealous of Genene's competence.

Dr. Robotham, Genene's one time ally, also started to

become suspicious of Genene when a six-month-old baby, Jose Antonio Flores, was admitted to the ICU with diarrhea, vomiting, and a fever; fairly common childhood symptoms. When placed under Genene's care, he suffered from unexplained seizures and went into cardiac arrest. Genene put a "code blue" into operation. The baby survived, and he seemed to be improving until the following day's 3 p.m. to 11 p.m. shift. Yet again, Jose suffered seizures and bleeding, and his heart stopped. This time, the doctors could not save him.

Later tests showed that he had had an overdose of heparin, an anticoagulant drug. No doctor had ordered it to be given to him. When it happened again to another child, a three-month-old boy named Albert Garza who survived, Dr. Robotham confronted Genene who angrily denied any wrong doing. Tighter controls were then introduced over the drug cabinet, in particular over access to heparin.

Dr. Robotham reported his suspicions about Genene to the hospital administration.

The administrators, not wanting a hospital scandal, decided that Dr. Robotham was over reacting. Sick babies died.

With Dr. Robotham and other doctors now complaining about Genene, her star nurse, Pat Belko began to take the rumors and gossip more seriously. Dr. Robothan and Pat Belko asked the hospital administrators to carry out an internal investigation.

## NURSES WHO MURDER

With several senior staff now requesting an investigation, the hospital administration was forced to begin an internal inquiry to see if one of its nurses was killing her patients. As the investigation got under way, patients in the pediatric ICU continued to suffer from unexplained medical problems and in some cases died. Patients, who had seemed stable, inexplicably stopped breathing or had heart seizures. Nearly all happened on the three-to-eleven shift. Dr. Robotham demanded that Genene be fired.

The financially strapped, struggling hospital lacking definitive proof of wrongdoing, fearful of an expensive lawsuit, and bad publicity, was unwilling to fire Genene or call in the district attorney. Without definite facts, firing Genene or calling the district attorney would put the hospital on shaky legal ground, as so far the inquiry had nothing but circumstantial evidence to link her to the incidents in the ICU. Genene could sue them and possibly win. Bexar County Hospital was also deeply concerned with its public image. It was desperate to generate paying patients to cover the costs of the poor and disadvantaged charity cases the hospital was supposedly created to accept. It didn't need the bad publicity a law suit would bring.

Months later, the inquiry found that between the months of May and December of 1981 ten children in the pediatric ICU had died after "sudden and unexplained" complications. In all cases, Genene was present and involved in the child's care. The report concluded: "This association of Nurse Jones with the deaths of the ten children could be coincidental. However, negligence or wrongdoing cannot be excluded." They never did anything with the report as Genene had left the hospital.

The administrators decided the simplest way around the problem was to only allow qualified RNs to work in the ICU as part of an upgrade to more professional care.

Pat Belko's boss, Ms. Mousseau, called a meeting of all the nurses on the pediatric ICU and broke the news to them. Apart from Genene, there were six other LVNs working on the unit, one of whom had worked there since 1969. They were told that they would all be offered other jobs in the hospital and if they decided to leave the hospital, they would all be given good references. They had until March 22nd to leave the ICU. Genene was offered another job at the hospital but was told that there were no other available pediatric positions. She resigned and left the hospital's employ on March 17th, 1982.

The administrators of the hospital were relieved. To them, the problem was solved. The medical emergencies on the three-to-eleven shift returned to normal numbers, and the "unexplained medical events" stopped.

Genene was unperturbed. She had been offered a job from Dr. Kathleen Holland, who she had befriended at Bexar Hospital. Dr. Holland was opening up a new pediatrics clinic in Kerrville, Texas 58 miles (93 km) northwest of San Antonio.

# NURSES WHO MURDER

## DR HOLLAND'S CLINIC

Kathy Holland began a three-year pediatric residency at Bexar County Hospital in July of 1979, shortly after she had divorced her first husband. She developed a reputation at the hospital as being capable and hardworking. Kathy decided that when she finished her residency, she wanted to have her own private pediatrics practice.

She decided she would open it in Kerrville, a small city in the Texas Hill Country, which was approximately sixty miles northwest of San Antonio. The downtown area of Kerrville is an historical site on the banks of the Guadalupe River. The city had long been a popular place for retirees but recently, according to Cathy's research, it had a growing population of young families and only one pediatrician. The city had a large general hospital, the Sid Peterson Memorial Hospital, but was weak in pediatrics. Dr. Holland thought that she would do well in Kerrville and fill a much needed gap in the market.

Dr. Holland was starting her new practice on a budget and needed to find a good nurse to help her. She didn't think she could afford an RN nurse as their wages were about $8.35 an hour whereas LVN wages were about $5 an hour. Dr. Holland had worked with Genene a few times at Bexar Hospital and had been impressed with her. She had heard that Genene "could stick an IV in a fly," and that was what Kathy Holland needed: a nurse with good technical skills who wasn't afraid to draw blood on children less than two years old.

Kathy Holland had heard the suspicions about Genene that she might be doing something to harm the children in the ICU unit, but she had worked with Genene and didn't believe it and so offered Genene a job at her new clinic. Dr. Robotham learned that Kathy had offered Genene a job and told Kathy she should think twice and voiced his suspicions to her.

Kathy Holland finished her residency at Bexar County on June 30th, 1982. By this time, she had received a very favorable reference for Genene from Bexar County Hospital. The hospital had even offered Genene another job. This convinced Kathy that all the gossip about Genene was just that: malicious gossip. The hospital administrators would hardly offer Genene another job or write her such a glowing reference if they thought she was harming patients, would they?

In July, Kathy Holland moved to Kerrville to set up her new practice. She bought a small three-bedroom house on Nixon Lane on the outskirts of the city and some land in the hills. Here, she intended to build a house once the practice had become successful. She hired a thirty-three-year-old woman, Gwen Grantner, as a secretary-receptionist. Genene Jones and her children moved to Kerrville and rented rooms from Kathy in the house on Nixon Lane.

Kathy Holland excitedly opened her new pediatric clinic on August 23rd, 1982. She gave Genene the title of pediatric clinician.

## NURSES WHO MURDER

The young parents of Kerrville were delighted that a new modern pediatric facility had opened in town.

### CHELSEA McCLELLAN

The first mother to take her child there was Petti McClellan. Petti had phoned earlier in the morning to make an appointment for her eight-month-old daughter Chelsea. Gwen Grantner gave her a 1.p.m appointment. Chelsea had been born four weeks prematurely, at the Sid Peterson Hospital, and had spent time on a respirator in the hospital's neonatal ICU. Due of this, Petti was extra protective of Chelsea. When she developed a heavy cold, she decided to take her to the new doctor in town to be checked over.

When Petti and her blond, pretty, blue-eyed daughter Chelsea arrived at the clinic, Gwen Grantner showed them into the doctor's office. The doctor had with her a small, plump nurse with green eyes, short, red-brown hair, with hard features that were dominated by a large nose. Dr. Holland introduced herself to Petti and then introduced her nurse, Genene Jones.

As is routine with a new patient, Dr. Holland wanted to know Chelsea's medical history. As Petti filled Dr. Holland in on her daughter's history, the baby began to get restless. Genene offered to take Chelsea next door while her mother talked to the doctor. Petti and Dr. Holland thought it was a good idea.

Five minutes later, Genene called for Dr. Holland to come quickly to the treatment room. Dr. Holland excused herself from

Petti and left her office shutting the door behind her. She went to find Genene in the treatment room and found Chelsea limp on the examining bed with Genene placing an oxygen mask over her face. Dr. Holland asked Genene to fit an IV in her scalp to insert an anticonvulsant drug, Dilantin, into her. Dr. Holland also asked Gwen Grantner to call the County Emergency Medical Service (EMS). Dr. Holland then went to her office and told Petti that her daughter had just had a seizure.

The emergency ambulance drew up outside the clinic at 1:25 p.m. Genene carried the baby into the ambulance, and the ambulance crew carried the IV bottle. Petti and Dr. Holland joined them. They arrived at Sid Peterson hospital minutes later where Chelsea was immediately admitted into the ICU. Chelsea remained there for nine days while the doctors carried out tests. The hospital was at a loss to explain the cause of the respiratory arrest and seizure. Chelsea survived.

Petti and her husband Reid McClellan believed that Genene had saved their child with her swift actions. The McClellans sang the praises of the new clinic to all their friends.

**BRANDY LEE BENITES**

On Friday the 27th of August, parents Nelda and Gabriel Benites were worried about their new one-month-old daughter Brandy Lee. She had been suffering from diarrhea for two days, and there was blood in her stool. They took her to Sid Peterson Hospital, and the hospital advised them to take her to the new pediatric clinic run by Dr. Holland. The doctor and the nurse Genene Jones took down notes of Brandy's history before removing her to the treatment room to be examined. Then Dr. Holland told the waiting parents that Brandy had stopped breathing and had suffered a seizure. Dr. Holland asked Gwen Grantner to call the County Emergency Medical Service (EMS). The ambulance arrived and took the baby, Genene, Nelda, and Gabriel Benites to Sid Peterson Hospital. Dr. Holland followed the ambulance in her car.

After half an hour at the Sid Peterson hospital, Dr. Holland told the parents she wanted the baby transferred to the San Antonio Santa Rosa Hospital. Another ambulance was called. As before, Genene and the baby, along with Brandy's mother, travelled in the ambulance with Dr. Holland and Mr. Benites following by car. Brandy Benites remained at the hospital in San Antonio for six days undergoing tests. The Doctors were unable to determine what had caused her seizure.

### CHRISTOPHER PARKER

On Monday, August 30th, Mary Ann Parker brought her four-month-old son Christopher to see Dr. Holland. Christopher suffered from raspy breathing, an illness known as *stridor* caused by constriction of the air passages. While Dr. Holland talked to Mary Parker, Genene took Christopher to be checked over. While he was with her, he started suffering respiratory problems.

# GENENE JONES

Dr. Holland had Gwen Grantner call an ambulance, and Christopher was taken to the hospital emergency room of Sid Peterson. While overseeing Christopher in the emergency room, another child, Jimmy Pearson, was admitted to the ward. Jimmy suffered from a heart defect known as a *Tetralogy of Fallot*. The little boy was suffering from seizures and was blue from lack of oxygen. The nurses on duty consulted with Dr. Holland who, after consulting with two of Jimmy's doctors in San Antonio, felt he should be moved by helicopter to the Santa Rosa hospital in San Antonio. Dr. Holland decided that Christopher should also be taken to the Santa Rosa hospital.

The helicopter, with two paramedics, took Jimmy, Christopher, and his nurse Genene aboard the helicopter. For fifteen minutes, all was calm until Genene began yelling over the noise of the helicopter engines that she thought Jimmy was having a seizure. The paramedics could see no change in his condition. Genene, according to the paramedics, then injected Jimmy with something into his IV line. A few minutes later, the paramedics said the equipment hooked up to Jimmy began showing heart irregularities, and he began to turn blue and stopped breathing. The paramedics revived him and diverted the helicopter to the Methodist Hospital where Jimmy was transferred to the emergency room and stabilized. The helicopter then continued its journey to the Santa Rosa hospital with Christopher and Genene.

Jimmy died seven weeks later.

# NURSES WHO MURDER

## MISTY REICHENAU

On Friday, September 3rd, Kay Reichenau called Dr. Holland's clinic to make an appointment as her normal family doctor, Duan Packard, was away on vacation. Her twenty-one-month-old daughter, Misty Reichenau, had a fever, a cold, and mouth sores causing her to stop eating and drinking. Gwen Grantner offered Mrs. Reichenau a 2 p.m. appointment.

Misty sat on her mother's knee as Kathy Holland examined her. She suspected it might possibly be a case of meningitis. Dr. Holland thought it was best to transfer Misty to the hospital for a spinal tap to test for the disease. Dr. Holland asked Genene to set up an IV for Misty as she also seemed dehydrated. Dr. Holland left the treatment room to phone the hospital, and Mrs. Reichenau went to telephone her husband Larry.

Another nurse, Debbie Sultenfuss, a friend of Genene's who occasionally helped out at the clinic, was there that day. When Kay Reichenau went back to the treatment room, Genene had the IV prepared. Baby Misty was crying loudly as Genene inserted liquid into it and then she went silent. Genene and Dr. Holland asked Kay to leave the room. Misty had stopped breathing and had gone into a seizure. An ambulance was sent for and Genene, Misty, and Kay were taken to the Sid Peterson hospital. Dr. Holland followed in her car. On arriving at the hospital, Genene carried Misty Reichenau up to the ICU. Dr. Holland told Mr. and Mrs. Reichenau that she wanted to transfer Misty to San Antonio to the Medical Center Hospital for further tests. Upon arrival there, the pediatric specialist, Dr. Ray Mackey, carried out various tests that failed to reveal the cause of the seizure. After five days, Misty was allowed to return home.

## CHELSEA McCLELLAN

On the morning of September 17th, Petti McClellan brought her two children Chelsea and Cameron to Dr. Holland's clinic. Her son Cameron had a cold, and Chelsea was due for inoculations.

Kathy Holland asked Genene to prepare the inoculations. Peti took Chelsea into the treatment room and had her sit on her knee. Genene administered the first injection into the baby's left thigh and within seconds Chelsea appeared to be having trouble breathing. Peti was alarmed and asked Genene to hold off giving the second shot, but Genene was insistent. The second injection she inserted into the baby's right thigh. Chelsea turned blue and stopped breathing. Gwen Grantner called for an ambulance while Dr. Holland inserted a breathing tube into Chelsea. Genene rode in the ambulance with Peti and Chelsea. Dr. Holland followed in her car. By the time they reached the hospital ten minutes later, Chelsea was breathing by herself. Dr. Holland thought that to be on the safe side, Chelsea should be transferred for neurological tests in San Antonio at the Santa Rosa Hospital.

Shortly after midday, an ambulance arrived at the Sid

## NURSES WHO MURDER

Peterson hospital. Genene, Chelsea, and a paramedic rode in the back of the ambulance, Kathy Holland followed in her car, while Peti and her husband Reid, a large black haired man with a shaggy moustache, followed in their own car.

In the ambulance, baby Chelsea was on a drip, and her heart was being monitored. Ten miles into the journey, Chelsea went into arrest. Genene ordered the ambulance to pull over saying the baby had "flat-lined!" Dr. Holland joined them in the ambulance and began massaging the baby's heart. Dr Holland then ordered the ambulance driver to take them to the nearest hospital. Upon arriving at the small, one-story Comfort Community Hospital, they rushed the baby into the emergency room, but little Chelsea was dead. Genene removed the tubes and cleaned the baby up and then wrapped her tiny body in a shawl and gave her to her mother. Dr. Holland was visibly upset and could not understand what had happened. She ordered an autopsy. The results from the autopsy took a few weeks, but the conclusion was that Chelsea had died of Sudden Infant Death Syndrome.

### JACOB EVANS

Just three hours after Chelsea's death, Genene was back at the clinic. Lydia Evans brought in her son, Jacob. Lydia was a nervous first time mother and was worried as her five-month-old son seemed to be crying so much. Genene said she wanted to do some blood tests and to also insert an IV. Lydia asked why she wanted to insert an IV. Genene said it was a precaution in case he had a seizure while they were running the tests. Lydia felt that was strange but presumed the nurse knew what she was doing.

Barely ten minutes after leaving Jacob in the treatment room with Genene, Jacob had a seizure. Gwen Grantner telephoned for an ambulance and phoned the hospital to page Kathy Holland. Once at the hospital, Jacob stabilized. He remained at the hospital for six days while the doctors tried to determine what had caused the seizure. They came up with no explanation.

The numbers of emergencies being sent to Sid Peterson hospital from Dr. Holland's new clinic had not gone unnoticed. Since the clinic had opened, the hospital emergency room was having as many as three children in it at a time. This was something that had never been seen before; something had to be wrong. There were also complaints from the ICU nurses about Genene's bossiness and interference.

Sid Peterson's administrator, Tony Hall, called a meeting of his top doctors and the head nurse of the ICU to discuss the matter. They all agreed that there was something not right. Tony Hall arranged an appointment with Dr. Holland to discuss the matter.

**ROLINDA RUFF**

On Thursday September 23rd', Clarabelle Ruff took her daughter Rolinda to Dr. Holland's clinic. The five-month-old girl had been suffering from diarrhea for two weeks. Dr. Holland said that Rolinda was suffering from dehydration, and she needed to be put on an IV line to replace lost fluids. Dr. Holland asked her nurse Genene to set one up. Genene then took Rolinda into the treatment room. Ten minutes later, Rolinda had stopped breathing. Gwen Grantner telephoned for an ambulance and warned the hospital that a code blue was on its way.

Word quickly spread around the Sid Peterson Hospital that there was yet another code blue coming from Dr. Holland's clinic. This was the eighth code blue in thirty-one days. This time when Genene and Dr. Holland arrived at the ICU with Rolinda, there were a number of other doctors there as well. An anesthesiologist, Dr. Frank Bradley, observed closely. He almost immediately recognized that Rolinda was coming out of the effects of a drug called ANECITNE. *ANECITNE, ALSO KNOWN AS* succinylcholine chloride, is a short-acting powerful muscle relaxant for intravenous (IV) administration that can debilitate a person's normal breathing response.

### SUSPICIONS CONFIRMED

Dr. Bradley confided his opinion quietly to the other doctors and reported to Tony Hall, Sid Peterson's administrator. In the meantime, another doctor had heard about the large number of baby deaths at the ICU where Genene had previously worked. This was also reported to Tony Hall. An emergency meeting was called for the following day after the interview with Dr. Holland.

## GENENE JONES

On Friday, September 24th, Dr. Holland found herself being interviewed by the top doctors at the hospital and *THE* administrator Tony Hall. She was asked why she thought so many children were getting sick at her clinic. Kathy Hall went through her notes one by one explaining each of the children's symptoms and the treatments she had performed. She was asked if she ever used *Anectine*. She said no. She was asked if she had any in the clinic. Kathy said yes, but she never used it. She was then asked about Genene Jones and did she know about the incidents at the pediatric ICU in San Antonio. She told the doctors that the hospital had given Genene a glowing reference. As the doctors fired their questions at her, Kathy began to feel sick. Had she made a dreadful mistake in hiring Genene?

Following the interview with Kathy Holland, the doctors held their meeting. They decided a proper investigation needed to be carried out and that in the meantime Dr. Holland was not to be allowed to treat any more patients at the Sid Peterson's hospital. They also decided that the law enforcement agents needed to be notified.

When Kathy Holland returned to her clinic on Monday September 27th, while Genene was out on her lunch break, she conducted an inventory of the drugs in the clinic. She examined the two bottles of Anectine; one of them had pinprick holes in the rubber stopper. Yet again, Kathy felt sick. When Genene returned from her lunch break, Kathy told her about her inquisition at the hospital and asked her to explain the pinpricks in the rubber stopper. Genene said the pinpricks had nothing to do with her.

When the bottle of *Anectine* was later analyzed, the contents were found to have been replaced with a saline solution. Kathy fired Genene Jones thirty odd days after opening her practice. Dr. Holland offered all the help she could give to the hospital investigation. She realized she had been naïve and stupid to trust Genene.

A grand jury in Kerr County on October 12, 1982 indicted Genene Jones on one count of murder and injury to seven other children. Genene was arrested and held in Kerr County jail.

Chelsea's parents, Reid and Petti McClellan, named Dr. Kathy Holland and Genene Jones in a wrongful death suit.

Another grand jury in San Antonio was assembled to look into a total of forty-seven children's suspicious deaths at Bexar County Medical Center Hospital. They had all occurred over a four year period that coincided with Genene Jones's time at the hospital. In November, the grand jury indicted Genene Jones for injuring Rolando Santos with a deliberate injection of heparin. She was suspected in the deaths of other infants, but the administrating staff at the hospital had destroyed pharmaceutical records, destroying the evidence needed to indict her and thus avoiding lawsuits that could potentially have been brought against the hospital.

Genene Jones had two separate trials. The first trial was for the killing of Chelsea McClellan and injury to seven other children.

## GENENE JONES

The prosecution claimed that Genene suffered from a hero complex; that she needed to make the children severely ill so that she could be seen as their savior by bringing them back to health; that she craved the excitement and attention the emergency she had created brought. On the other hand, her defense team tried to prove that Genene was a competent, devoted, and responsible nurse. The jury was only out for three hours before they returned on February 15$^{th}$, 1984 with a guilty verdict. Genene cried as the verdict was read out. The judge sentenced Genene Jones to ninety-nine years in prison.

The trial cost Kerr County a big part of its annual court budget.

Much of the same evidence was repeated in her second trial for injuring Rolando Santos in October of 1984. In this trial, Genene, who was age thirty-three, was also found guilty and sentenced to a concurrent term of sixty years in prison; the two sentences totaling 159 years in all.

Genene Jones came up for a parole hearing in 1994; it was denied. Since then, she has applied for parole six times; all of them have been denied. She is set to be released in 2017 at the age of sixty-six.

Dr. Kathy Holland still runs a pediatrician clinic in Kerrville. The parents of Chris Parker and Brandy Benites continued to use her clinic after Genene's conviction.

Chelsea's parents, Reid and Petti McClellan, were furious

and incredulous at the administrators of Bexar County Medical Center Hospital not warning anyone about their suspicions of Genene and their total irresponsibility at giving Genene a reference thus allowing her to continue killing babies. They remain unconvinced that Dr. Holland was unaware of what Genene was up to.

Genene Jones was portrayed in a television movie Deadly Medicine (1991) by the actress Susan Ruttan. It is rumored that she inspired the character Annie Wilkes in Stephen King's book *Misery*.

Like Reid and Petti McClellan, I am astounded at the actions of the Bexar County Medical Center Hospital. More important to them than protecting the public and innocent babies from a serial killer was their reputation and fear of law suits.

# BEVERLY ALLITT

Beverley Gail Allitt was born on the 4th of October in 1968, in England as one of four children. As a small child, she appeared happy but as she grew, she began to wear bandages and dressings over wounds she refused to allow anyone to examine. Her parents felt it was all due to attention seeking. As she entered puberty, she became overweight and increasingly sought attention. Beverly also began to show aggressive tendencies. Beverley also complained increasingly of physical pains that had her parents constantly taking her to the hospital with symptoms such as headaches, pains in the gall bladder, uncontrolled vomiting, urinary infections, blurred vision, appendicitis, back pains, and ulcers, to mention just a few. She faked her appendix symptoms so well, she ended up having a perfectly normal, healthy appendix removed. This ended up being extremely slow to heal as Beverly kept picking at the surgical wound. Doctor's soon began to see her attention-seeking behavior.

After Beverly left school, she began training to become a nurse. During her training, she was frequently sick due to claiming a variety of illnesses. Her fellow students suspected her of odd behavior, such as smearing feces on a wall and in a nursing establishment where she undertook her training, leaving excrement in the fridge. A boyfriend of hers at this time later reported that she was deceptive, manipulative, and violent. Before their relationship had ended, she had claimed a false pregnancy and rape. He thought he was well rid of her. Unsurprisingly, due to her poor attendance; she failed many of her nursing examinations. Despite this, she was given in early 1991, at the age of 23, a six-month contract at the critically understaffed NHS hospital of Grantham and Kesteven, in Lincolnshire. She began work in Ward 4, a children's ward. When Beverly began working at the hospital, only two properly qualified trained nurses were on the day shift and only one on the night shift.

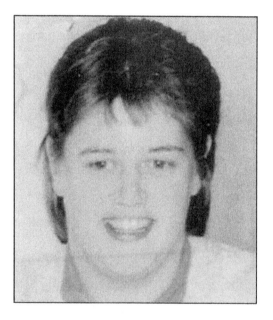

*Beverly Allitt*

# BEVERLY ALLITT

On February 21st, 1991 Liam Taylor, a seven-month-old baby was placed in Ward Four with a suspected chest infection. Nurse Beverly Alitt reassured his distraught parents that their son was in the best possible place to recover. She persuaded the parents that the best thing they could do for their child was to return home and get some sleep. The following morning when Mr. and Mrs. Taylor returned, Beverly told them that, in the night, Liam had suffered a respiratory problem but was now fine. She told the anxious parents that she would do an extra night's duty so she personally could keep an eye on their son. Mr. and Mrs. Taylor also decided to sleep that night in the hospital in a room kept for parents of small children.

That night, baby Liam suffered another respiratory complication but came through it to the doctor's satisfaction. Baby Liam was then alone with only Nurse Beverly Allitt in attendance. Another nurse appeared and noticed that Liam was deathly pale and then red patches surfaced on his little face. Beverly began yelling for an emergency team. The other nurses on duty were perplexed as to why the alarm monitors had not sounded when Liam had stopped breathing. Baby Liam Taylor suffered cardiac arrest. The attending doctors did all they could but even with all of their efforts, Liam suffered massive brain damage. The only thing now keeping the baby alive was the life-support machine that kept his lungs functioning. On the doctor's advice, because of the severe brain damage, Mr. and Mrs. Taylor agreed to have the life support turned off. Liam's death was attributed to heart failure. Beverley observed the whole drama before putting on her coat and going home. She returned to work later for her next night shift almost as if nothing had happened.

On March 5th, 1991 Timothy Hardwick, an eleven-year-old boy who suffered from cerebral palsy, was admitted to Ward 4 having had an epileptic fit. Nurse Beverly Allitt was on duty and took over his care. Within a few moments of being left alone with Timothy, she began yelling for help that Timothy was suffering a cardiac arrest. Other hospital staff ran to her aid including the emergency resuscitation team, who on reaching him found he had no pulse and was turning blue. Despite strenuous efforts by the medical team, Timothy died. An autopsy was carried out but failed to provide a clear cause of death and so his death was attributed to epilepsy.

On March 3rd, 1991, Kayley Desmond, a one-year-old little girl, was taken to Ward 4 suffering from an infection of the chest. She appeared to be responding well to treatment until five days later when she was left alone with Nurse Beverly Allitt. Kayley then suffered a cardiac arrest. The emergency team succeeded in reviving her, and she was moved to a Nottingham hospital. Here, during an extensive examination, a doctor found a needle mark under her armpit along with an air bubble close by. The doctor thought it was most likely caused by an accidental injection, and there was no investigation carried out.

# BEVERLY ALLITT

On March 20, 1991, Paul Crampton, a five-month-old boy, was admitted to Ward 4 with a bronchial infection that was not considered serious. Just before Paul was discharged, he was left alone with Nurse Beverly Allitt. Within minutes, Beverly was calling for help as the baby boy appeared to be suffering from insulin shock. On three separate occasions, Paul sank into a near-coma. On each occasion, the doctors managed to revive him, but they were puzzled by the fluctuations in his insulin levels. He was sent by ambulance, accompanied by Nurse Beverly Allitt, to the Nottingham hospital where on admission he was again fond to have too high levels of insulin. Paul survived.

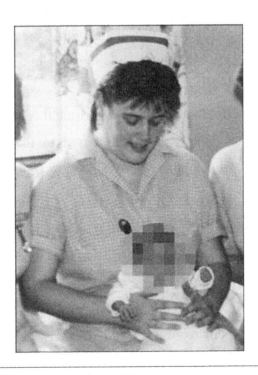

# NURSES WHO MURDER

The following day, Bradley Gibson, a 5-year-old boy who was in ward 4 suffering from pneumonia, suddenly experienced cardiac arrest. The emergency team of doctors saved him. They then ran some blood tests and were puzzled by his high levels of insulin. Later that night, when alone with Nurse Beverly Allitt, he suffered another cardiac arrest. Yet again, he was revived and then moved to the Nottingham hospital where he recovered. Extraordinarily, with all the unexplained and mystifying health events that all happened in Nurse Beverly Allitt's presence, no suspicions were aroused.

On March 22nd, 1991, a little two-year-old boy, Yik Hung Chan, who was on ward 4 after having fallen out of a window and fracturing his skull, was left alone with Nurse Beverly Allitt. He began to turn blue and appeared to be having some kind of attack. Beverly called for help, and the boy was revived with oxygen. A few hours later, Yik Hung Chan suffered another similar attack. After reviving him again, he was transferred to the bigger hospital in Nottingham. His symptoms were thought to be due to his fall.

Nurse Beverly Allitt then began to take an interest in two little twin baby girls, Katie and Becky Phillips. They were two-months-old and had been born prematurely and were being kept in the hospital for observation. After being allowed home, Becky Phillips was brought to Ward 4, on April 1st, 1991, suffering from gastroenteritis. On April 3rd, Nurse Beverly Allitt told doctors that she thought Becky was hypoglycemic and cold to the touch. On examination, the doctors found no ailment. Becky Phillips was discharged and sent home with her mother Sue Phillips.

That night, baby Becky cried out with what her parents thought was pain. A doctor visited the house and thought it was a case of colic. The parents slept that night with Becky in their bed where she died during the night. An autopsy was performed, but the pathologists found no obvious cause of death.

Katie Phillips, the surviving twin, was then admitted to Ward 4 as a precaution. Nurse Beverly Allitt assured the distraught mother that she would keep an extra special eye on Katie. Left alone with Beverly, baby Katie stopped breathing. The emergency team were called and managed to revive Katie. Sue Phillips attributed Katie's life being saved to Beverly. In gratitude, she asked Beverly to be Katie's godmother. Nurse Beverly Allitt graciously accepted the honor, as if she had been a hero.

Two days later, baby Katie suffered another attack which caused her lungs to collapse, and it was with considerable difficulty that the emergency team managed to revive her. Once revived, she was sent to Nottingham hospital. Here, the doctors on examining her discovered that five of her ribs were broken and that she had suffered severe brain damage due to oxygen deprivation.

Four more young victims followed but, fortunately, all were saved by being transferred to Nottingham hospital. The doctors at

## NURSES WHO MURDER

Nottingham's hospital were beginning to suspect that something was not entirely right at Grantham and Kesteven Hospital.

When a little girl, Claire Peck, a fifteen-month-old asthmatic patient who needed a breathing tube was alone with Nurse Beverly Allitt, she suffered a cardiac arrest. The emergency team managed to revive her. When left alone again with Beverly, she suffered another heart attack from which she died on April 22, 1991.

The autopsy examination showed that Claire Peck had died from natural causes. However, Dr. Nelson Porter, a consultant at the hospital was most unhappy at the high number of heart cases which had occurred over the past eight weeks on Ward 4 and began an investigation. At first, he thought that maybe it was caused by a virus in the ventilation system, but tests proved negative. Dr. Nelson Porter then called for more tests to be carried out on baby Claire. These tests showed abnormally high levels of potassium in the baby's blood and in her tissues there were traces of Lignocaine, a drug used to treat adults suffering from cardiac arrest and one that is never given to babies. The hospital called in the police.

Superintendent Stuart Clifton was put in charge of the investigation, and it didn't take too long to find the common thread in all the cases: Nurse Beverly Allitt. Within 3 weeks of starting the investigation, Superintendent Clifton arrested Nurse Beverly Allitt. Beverly strenuously denied any knowledge of the attacks. She said all she did was try and save lives. Sue Phillips, the twin's mother, so believed in Beverly that she hired a private investigator to clear Beverly's name; a decision she must now seriously regret. After several court hearings, Beverly was charged with eleven counts of causing grievous bodily harm, eleven counts of attempted murder, and four counts of murder. Beverly lost a large amount of weight and developed anorexia nervosa while in prison awaiting her trial. She was also examined by psychiatrists sent by the prosecution and defense teams.

Both sets of psychiatrists diagnosed Beverly as suffering from Munchausen syndrome: a form of severe factitious disorder where the sufferer makes up physical symptoms that are either false or self-induced. Sufferers are not malingering; they just want to play the patient role for attention. They also found her to be suffering from Munchausen by Proxy syndrome. This is when the sufferer harms others to gain attention for themselves.

After several delays caused by Beverly's "illnesses", Beverly Allitt's trial started on February 15th, 1993, at Nottingham's Crown Court. The trial lasted nearly two months and during it, Beverly only attended sixteen days due to her "illnesses". Beverly was found guilty of all charges. In May of 1993, Beverly was sentenced to thirteen life sentences. The judge, Mr. Justice Latham, told Beverly Allitt that he considered her "a serious danger" to others. He ordered her to be incarcerated at Rampton Hospital, a secure hospital in Nottinghamshire which houses among others those deemed criminally insane. Beverly Allitt has, since her detention, admitted to three of the infant murders and six of the assaults. Her earliest possible parole date is 2032 when she will be sixty-four.

# OTHER BOOKS BY SYLVIA PERRINI

### WOMEN SERIAL KILLERS OF THE 17th CENTURY (WOMEN WHO KILL)

ASIN:B00BKPWKG6

**ISBN-13:** 978-1482657807

This was the century when royal poison scandals sent shockwaves throughout Europe. The scandals so rocked France, that Louis XIV in 1662, passed a law stopping the sale of poisonous substances to people other than professionals, and for all purchasers to be registered.

In this short booklet of approximately 9,300 words, best selling author Sylvia Perrini takes a look at some of the most prolific women poisoners of this century, and a look at one woman, who did not use poison, just torture.

### WOMEN MURDERERS OF THE 18th CENTURY (WOMEN WHO KILL)

ASIN:B007B2G0KY

**ISBN-13:** 978-1482678642

Why do women kill and murder? They are supposed to be the gentler sex, the ones who nurture the babies and support families, keeping the very structure of society in place. Why do some women go wrong? Is it greed, jealousy, power or just plain wickedness?

Women Murderers have been around for centuries. In this short book of approximately 12,500 words best selling author Sylvia Perrini looks at the profiles of eight women who operated in the 18th century.

**WOMEN SERIAL KILLERS OF THE 19th CENTURY: THE GOLDEN AGE OF POISONS (WOMEN WHO KILL)**

ASIN:B00BK9QY2S

**ISBN-13:**978-1482696721

The 19th Century is often regarded as the heyday of poisoners. In the beginning to the middle of the nineteenth century, a poisoning panic engrossed the public imagination. In the Times newspaper in England, between 1830 and 1839, fifty-nine cases of murder by poisoning were reported. By the 1840s, the number reported had risen to hundreds. And, of these hundreds of poisonings, sixty percent involved women murderers.

In this fascinating book, best selling author Sylvia Perrini, looks at serial women killers around the world in the 19th Century. Nearly all the cases, but not all, involve poisoning.

**WOMEN SERIAL KILLERS OF THE 20th CENTURY**

ASIN:B00C0JRMFA

**ISBN-13:** 978-1483953960

The 20th-century, like the previous centuries, has seen no end of murders by women with poison as their choice of weapon. Furthermore, just like in the previous centuries, the murders have been just as cold and calculating.

Those lucky few who have managed to survive an attempted murder by these women have described being poisoned as being equal to being devoured alive.

However, the 20th century has also seen murders committed by women with guns and, in the case of Dana Gray, with physical violence. Dana is a rarity among women serial killers, in both her choice of victim and her hands-on method of using her hands, a cord or rope, and an object with which to batter her victim.

Yet, even after all this time, we are left with the same question: what leads a woman to commit serial murder?

In this book, Ms Perrini examines the profiles of twenty-five women serial killers, all of whom acted alone.

She has not included mothers who solely kill their own children as she believes that is a subject that deserves to be written about entirely separately.

Even leaving those specific types of Women Serial Killers aside, there are still many women who choose to commit murder again, and again, and again…

Welcome to the world of 20th century women serial killers.

OR BUY THE ABOVE FOUR BOOKS IN ONE

**WOMEN SERIAL KILLERS THROUGH TIME Boxed Set (4 in 1)**

**ISBN-13:** 978-1484044261

**BABY FARMERS OF THE 19th CENTURY (WOMEN WHO KILL)**

ASIN:B00ACPGTFI

**ISBN-13:** 978-1484128725

The practice of baby farming came about in late Victorian times. In this era, there was a great social stigma attached to having a child out of marriage and no adequate contraception existed. In this period of time, no child protection services or regulated adoption agencies were in existence.

A number of untrained women offered adoption and fostering services to unmarried mothers who would hand over their baby and a cash payment. The mothers hoped that this payment would find stable, happy homes for their babies. And in the case of weekly payments that they would at some time in the future be able to reclaim their child.

It was, without doubt, one of the most sickening aspects of Victorian times, not only in Britain but also in its colonies as well.

Many of these fostering and adoption agencies were bona fide, but a frightening number were not. They became known as baby farms.

In this short book, best selling author, Sylvia Perrini, introduces us to some of these baby farmers.

**FIVE WOMEN SERIAL KILLER PROFILES; Boxed Set**

ASIN: B00A9HW3KO

This is a compilation of best-selling author, Sylvia Perrini's, five short books of Women Serial Killers.

The profiles contained in this volume are:

DOROTHEA HELEN PUENTE-SOCIAL WORKER'S SAVIOR!!

VELMA BARFIELD- GATEWAY TO HEAVEN

GENENE JONES-CODE BLUE

AILEEN WUORNUS-DAMSEL FOR SALE

KATHLEEN FOLBIGG--UNJUST JUSTICE?

Some of these stories will shock you to the core, and some may make you weep. They may also be bought separately.

**NO, DAD! PLEASE, DON'T! (THE JOHN LIST**

STORY) (MURDER IN THE FAMILY)

**ASIN:**B00EI2BA28

On the morning of December the 8th, 1971, New Jersey, and indeed the entire metropolitan New York City area, awoke to lurid newspaper headlines of the horrific massacre of almost an entire family in the affluent community of Westfield, N.J.; a story that both captivated and horrified a nation. The story was quickly picked up around the world.

The face of John List, who had left letters confessing to the crime, stared out at the readers. He was an ordinary, fairly nondescript looking man. The question on everyone's lips as news broke of the horrific slaughter by a college-educated, seemingly successful accountant, and Sunday school teacher was why? He had murdered his mother, wife and three teenage children. In this short booklet, of approximately 11,000 words, best selling author, Sylvia Perrini, delves into the events that led to the horrific slaughter of John Lists, mother, wife and three teenage children.

John List managed to evade capture for over 18 years and never expressed remorse for his crimes.

# DEADLY DADS of the UK (PATERNAL FILICIDE)

**ASIN:** B00H14P5TY
**ISBN-13:** 978-1494762148

Of all the hideous violent crimes that are committed, the murder of one's own children, one's own flesh and blood, are the most baffling. We immediately presume the parent must have lost his mind in a temporary moment of insanity or madness. It is hardly surprising that we find ourselves recoiling in horror at such appalling tragedies and comfort ourselves by thinking that they are isolated, senseless, incidents.

What can possibly make a father commit such unspeakable savagery against his family? Is it despair, hatred, or revenge, or a hideous, deranged possessive love or an incomprehensible abnormality? Are these fathers normal men driven to the edge when circumstances in their lives go wrong or just devilish fiends?

Unfortunately, as demonstrated in the following profiles in this book, and there are a great many more than those the author has included, these kinds of murders are not as rare as we would like to believe.

**SERIAL KILLERS TRUE CRIME ANTHOLOGY 2014 (Annual Anthology)**

**Sylvia Perrini** (Author), Peter Vronsky (Author), Michael Newton (Author), RJ Parker (Author), Dane Ladwig (Author)

**ISBN-13:** 978-1494325893

**Publisher:** RJ PARKER PUBLISHING; First edition (December 15, 2013)

WARNING: This book contains forensic crime scene evidence photographs and statements that some may find disturbing.

Serial killers; they cross the bounds of evil. They murder at random without logic or reason other than the one twisting in their sick and evil minds. They are diabolical vile creatures devoid of morality or pity. You will meet a chosen few of them in these pages. We will see that serial killers are roaming among us all, from small towns to big cities. They are not limited to a particular place, gene pool, culture, social class or religion. They are not restricted to any particular demographic, political propensity and they can be of any gender.

Some of the serial killers chosen for this first annual Serial Killers True Crime Anthology you might have heard of and we present their tales in new ways. Others have not graced every newspaper, tabloid or television screen and represent tales of true crime horror told in detail for the first time in these pages. Five of true crime's most prolific authors have come together in these pages to present their most compelling cases of serial homicide, famous and not so famous.

# OTHER GOLDMINE GUIDE.COM PUBLICATIONS

## SAILING INTO THE ABYSS (TRUE SMUGGLING ADVENTURE) (MARIJUANA SMUGGLING) BRIDGET LANE

**ASIN:**B009N1IRSE

This is the true life story of a young English woman, who initially set out single-handedly to smuggle two tons of marijuana from Colombia to the US. It is a gripping story of battling storms, snakes, engine problems in Great White Shark infested waters, days at sea facing deprivations barely imaginable, and Mexican gun boats.

A journey that finally sees Bridget incarcerated in the most infamous prison in Mexico-La Mesa. This is truly an extraordinary adventure story of a remarkable woman operating in a man's world.

## WOMEN PIRATES (SCANDALOUS WOMEN)

## ANNA MYERS

**ASIN:**B007KQCBF4

There is an old superstition among sailors that women at sea bring bad luck. Despite this, many women have proved their seafaring skills. When we think of Pirates we have a tendency to think of masculine men. But did you know that the most successful pirate of all time was a woman? Neither the Chinese, British or Portuguese navies could stop her.

In this delightful short book author Anna Myers takes a look at the lives of eight wicked women pirates.

## DESERT QUEEN; LADY HESTER STANHOPE (SCANDALOUS WOMEN)

## ANNA MYERS

**ASIN:**B00BAKB4XQ

In this wonderful short book, author Anna Myers looks at the colorful life of the extraordinary bohemian adventuress Lady Hester Stanhope.

Lady Hester lived in England until the age of about 34 when she set off traveling and fell in love with the Middle East. While en route to Egypt she was shipwrecked, and lost all her clothes. Unable to purchase European clothes she adopted a male version of Turkish dress. This, made her a bit of a 'cause celeb' in the Middle East, and also that she rode horseback into Damascus without a veil, an unthinkable thing to do at the time. In fact, many of the things Lady Hester did were unthinkable at the time, which is what made her such a colorful character.

Many of the travels she undertook were exceedingly dangerous, but she appeared fearless. She was the first European woman - and one of the few Europeans to survive the dangerous journey - to enter Palmyra, in the middle of the Syrian desert. The native Bedouins crowned her as "Queen of the Desert". Hester chose to settle down in Lebanon, where she became a local folk hero, offering shelter to those affected by wars and the battles for supremacy in the region.

When the British Government, under Lord Palmerston, stopped her pension, she died in her home in Djoun, destitute, friendless and alone.

## SCANDALOUS LADIES (WICKED WOMEN)

## ANNA MYERS

**ASIN:** B007S9YCIM

Author Anna Myers in this delightful short book, provides a gallery of extraordinary women swindlers, con artists and imposters. Some of the women you may even like and some you will despise.

MARTHE HANAU

'La Banquière'

POILLON SISTERS

Sisters you wouldn't want to meet on a dark night.

ELIZABETH BIGLEY

The Enterprising Mrs. Chadwick

THÉRÈSE HUMBERT

ANN O'DELIA DISS DEBAR

"One of the most extraordinary fake mediums and mystery swindlers the world has ever known".

ANNA SCHNEIDER

Too Many Husbands Spoil The Broth

ELLEN PECK

Just never wanted to retire!

BERTHA HEYMAN

"One of the smartest confidence women in America"

SARAH RACHEL RUSSELL

'The Beautician from Hell'

SARAH WILSON

Princess of Mecklenburg-Strelitz sister?

ANNA ANDERSON

Was she Czar Nicolas's II daughter ?

PRINCESS CARABOO

The greatest actress of all time!

**LOVE YOUR LIVER:How to keep your liver healthy (HEALTHY LIVING) PENNY LANE**

**ASIN:**B0077SP1SO

This book has some great tips for good liver health, delicious liver-friendly recipes and information that will help you get to know one of your most hardworking and vital organs. The liver performs an amazing 500 different functions. It produces bile, essential for breaking down fat for absorption and extracting vitamins A, D, E and K, stores energy from food until it is needed, and aids our natural immunity by releasing chemicals to fight infection. With so many important jobs to do, your liver is robust enough to carry on even when it is damaged - it can even repair itself. But every organ has its limits and the liver is no exception. We must learn to love our liver. Our liver helps us to recover from all our over indulgence's So learn to give your liver the love it deserves, and this book will help you do so.

## FISH AND SEAFOOD FOR LOVE (NATURE'S NATURAL APRODISIACS)

**ASIN:B00DKE6TLM**

The ancient world believed seafood had aphrodisiac characteristics because, the Greek goddess of love, Aphrodite, sprang from the foam of the sea on an oyster shell (hence Botticelli's much reproduced painting of the goddess floating on a seashell). The Romans named her Venus.

The sea is one of the major sources of life and Seafood has been seen as the food of love for many centuries. A claim that is not surprising considering it is brimming with minerals such as calcium, zinc, iodine and iron.

In this delightful book of aphrodisiac foods, the author looks at the most popular fishy aphrodisiacs as well as providing some excellent recipes to enjoy them.

CPSIA information can be obtained
at www.ICGtesting.com
Printed in the USA
LVOW04s1418241115
463965LV00020B/181/P